W9-BUI-559

DATE DUE

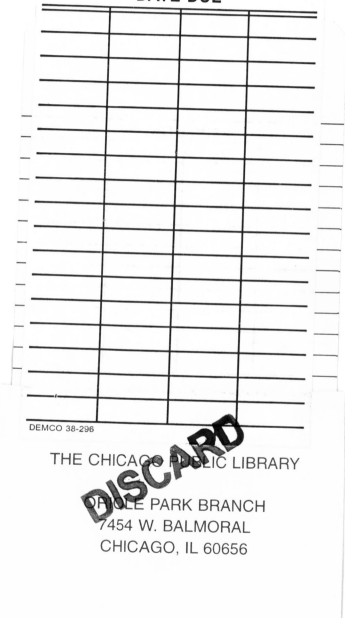

DEMCO 38-296

The Oklahoma City Bombing

The Oklahoma City Bombing

Hal Marcovitz

CHELSEA HOUSE PUBLISHERS
Philadelphia

Frontispiece: Pieces of the Alfred P. Murrah Federal Building spill into the street after a bomb explosion ripped open the front of the building on April 19, 1995, in Oklahoma City, Oklahoma.

CHELSEA HOUSE PUBLISHERS

Editor in Chief Sally Cheney
Director of Production Kim Shinners
Creative Manager Takeshi Takahashi
Manufacturing Manager Diann Grasse

Staff for THE OKLAHOMA CITY BOMBING

Assistant Editor Susan Naab
Picture Researcher Jaimie Winkler
Production Assistant Jaimie Winkler
Series Designer Takeshi Takahashi
Cover Designer: Keith Trego
Layout 21st Century Publishing and Communications, Inc.

First Printing

1 3 5 7 9 8 6 4 2

The Chelsea House World Wide Web address is
http://www.chelseahouse.com

Library of Congress Cataloging-in-Publication Data

Marcovitz, Hal.
  The Oklahoma City bombing / by Hal Marcovitz.
    p. cm. — (Great disasters, reforms and ramifications)
Summary: Details the events surrounding the 1995 terrorist bombing of the federal building in Oklahoma City, as well as the investigation and trial of those responsible for the blast and the execution of Timothy McVeigh.
Includes bibliographical references and index.
  ISBN 0-7910-6738-6 (hardcover) — ISBN 0-7910-6912-5 (pbk.)
  1. Oklahoma City Federal Building Bombing, Oklahoma City, Okla., 1995—Juvenile literature. 2. McVeigh, Timothy —Juvenile literature. 3. Terrorism—Oklahoma—Oklahoma City—Juvenile literature. 4. Bombings—Oklahoma—Oklahoma City—Juvenile literature. 5. Right-wing extremists—United States—Juvenile literature. [1. Oklahoma City Federal Building Bombing, Oklahoma City, Okla., 1995. 2. McVeigh, Timothy. 3. Terrorism.] I. Title. II. Series.
HV6432 .M365 2002
364.16'4—dc21
2001008382

Contents

GREAT DISASTERS
REFORMS and RAMIFICATIONS

THE *APOLLO 1* AND *CHALLENGER* DISASTERS

BHOPAL

THE BLACK DEATH

THE BLIZZARD OF 1888

THE BOMBING OF HIROSHIMA

THE CHERNOBYL NUCLEAR DISASTER

THE DUST BOWL

THE EXPLOSION OF TWA FLIGHT 800

THE *EXXON VALDEZ*

THE GALVESTON HURRICANE

THE GREAT CHICAGO FIRE

THE GREAT PLAGUE AND FIRE OF LONDON

THE *HINDENBURG*

THE HOLOCAUST

THE INFLUENZA PANDEMIC OF 1918

THE IRISH POTATO FAMINE

THE JOHNSTOWN FLOOD

LOVE CANAL

THE MUNICH OLYMPICS

NUCLEAR SUBMARINE DISASTERS

THE OKLAHOMA CITY BOMBING

PEARL HARBOR

THE SALEM WITCH TRIALS

THE SAN FRANCISCO EARTHQUAKE OF 1906

THE SPANISH INQUISITION

THE STOCK MARKET CRASH OF 1929

TERRORISM

THREE MILE ISLAND

THE *TITANIC*

THE TRIANGLE SHIRTWAIST COMPANY FIRE OF 1911

THE WACO SIEGE

THE WORLD TRADE CENTER BOMBING

Jill McCaffrey
National Chairman
Armed Forces Emergency Services
American Red Cross

Introduction

D isasters have always been a source of fascination and awe. Tales of a great flood that nearly wipes out all life are among humanity's oldest recorded stories, dating at least from the second millennium B.C., and they appear in cultures from the Middle East to the Arctic Circle to the southernmost tip of South America and the islands of Polynesia. Typically gods are at the center of these ancient disaster tales—which is perhaps not too surprising, given the fact that the tales originated during a time when human beings were at the mercy of natural forces they did not understand.

To a great extent, we still are at the mercy of nature, as anyone who reads the newspapers or watches nightly news broadcasts can attest.

Hurricanes, earthquakes, tornados, wildfires, and floods continue to exact a heavy toll in suffering and death, despite our considerable knowledge of the workings of the physical world. If science has offered only limited protection from the consequences of natural disasters, it has in no way diminished our fascination with them. Perhaps that's because the scale and power of natural disasters force us as individuals to confront our relatively insignificant place in the physical world and remind us of the fragility and transience of our lives. Perhaps it's because we can imagine ourselves in the midst of dire circumstances and wonder how we would respond. Perhaps it's because disasters seem to bring out the best and worst instincts of humanity: altruism and selfishness, courage and cowardice, generosity and greed.

As one of the national chairmen of the American Red Cross, a humanitarian organization that provides relief for victims of disasters, I have had the privilege of seeing some of humanity's best instincts. I have witnessed communities pulling together in the face of trauma; I have seen thousands of people answer the call to help total strangers in their time of need.

Of course, helping victims after a tragedy is not the only way, or even the best way, to deal with disaster. In many cases planning and preparation can minimize damage and loss of life—or even avoid a disaster entirely. For, as history repeatedly shows, many disasters are caused not by nature but by human folly, shortsightedness, and unethical conduct. For example, when a land developer wanted to create a lake for his exclusive resort club in Pennsylvania's Allegheny Mountains in 1880, he ignored expert warnings and cut corners in reconstructing an earthen dam. On May 31, 1889, the dam gave way, unleashing 20 million tons of water on the towns below. The Johnstown Flood, the deadliest in American history, claimed more than 2,200 lives. Greed and negligence would figure prominently in the Triangle Shirtwaist Company fire in 1911. Deplorable conditions in the garment sweatshop, along with a failure to give any thought to the safety of workers, led to the tragic deaths of 146 persons. Technology outstripped wisdom only a year later, when the designers of the luxury liner *Titanic* smugly declared their state-of-the-art ship "unsinkable," seeing no need to provide lifeboat capacity for everyone onboard. On the night of April 14, 1912, more than 1,500 passengers and crew paid for this hubris with their lives after the ship collided with an iceberg and sank. But human catastrophes aren't always the unforeseen consequences of carelessness or folly. In the 1940s the leaders of Nazi Germany purposefully and systematically set out to exterminate all Jews, along with Gypsies, homosexuals, the mentally ill, and other so-called undesirables. More recently terrorists have targeted random members of society, blowing up airplanes and buildings in an effort to advance their political agendas.

The books in the GREAT DISASTERS: REFORMS AND RAMIFICATIONS series examine these and other famous disasters, natural and human made. They explain the causes of the disasters, describe in detail how events unfolded, and paint vivid portraits of the people caught up in dangerous circumstances. But these books are more than just accounts of what happened to whom and why. For they place the disasters in historical perspective, showing how people's attitudes and actions changed and detailing the steps society took in the wake of each calamity. And in the end, the most important lesson we can learn from any disaster—as well as the most fitting tribute to those who suffered and died—is how to avoid a repeat in the future.

Difficult
Days Ahead

Physical trials, both successes and setbacks, characterized Timothy McVeigh's experience with the United States Army. His superiors decorated him with honors for his service during the Gulf War and his performance afterward.

Sergeant Timothy McVeigh fell exhausted onto his bunk; he was tired, drenched with sweat, and his feet were blistered. He had gone out on the five-mile hike with new boots. It was a mistake; the stiff leather irritated his feet, and the old military remedies of changing socks and spraying his feet with antiperspirant hadn't worked.

Although his feet bothered him the most, the rest of his body ached as well. The tall, rail-thin soldier arrived at Fort Bragg in North Carolina just two days before, following a long and tiring journey from Saudi Arabia in the Persian Gulf more than 6,000 miles away. The trip had been grueling. McVeigh and a buddy had hopped from military plane to military plane, making stops in Spain and Newfoundland, Canada, before landing in Connecticut, where they found seats on a commercial airliner bound for North Carolina. They hadn't even had time for showers before they arrived at Fort Bragg.

What's more, McVeigh had spent three months in the Persian Gulf as a gunner aboard a Bradley Fighting Vehicle, a light tank that was particularly effective in desert warfare because it was able to skip swiftly over the miles of endless sand dunes in Saudi Arabia and Kuwait. McVeigh's unit had been called to duty for Operation Desert Storm, the United Nations' offensive to drive the Iraqis out of Kuwait. Conditions in the Persian Gulf were hard on McVeigh and the other American soldiers. During the day, the temperatures soared well above 100 degrees; at night, the cold desert conditions would drop the thermometer down to near freezing.

William Dilly, who served with McVeigh in the Gulf, recalled it was difficult for the Americans to keep in shape because the harsh desert conditions were not conducive to physical training, known as "PT" in the military. "We would do jumping jacks and try, but we couldn't run," Dilly said. "We could do no running because of the sand. We would do approximately 15 minutes of PT in the morning. So he was not in very good condition."

McVeigh served well in Operation Desert Storm. His toughness, dedication, and valor had been recognized by his commanders, who recommended him for Army Special Forces. Known as the "Green Berets," Special Forces soldiers are members of the Army's elite unit of fighting men—commandos given only the most dangerous assignments.

The Army regards its Special Forces soldiers as "a breed apart, a cut above the rest . . . mature, highly skilled, superbly trained . . . a fighter of uncommon physical and mental caliber, ready to serve anywhere at any time."

Timothy McVeigh occupied the dangerous position of gunner in a Bradley Fighting Vehicle unit, often the first military presence on the battlefield because they easily crossed the desert sand. The mask protects the gunner's face in colder weather.

Although similar commandos have fought for America as far back as the War for Independence, Special Forces traces its history to 1952 when the unit was formed under Colonel Aaron Bank. The unit fought first in the Korean War; later, Special Forces soldiers played an integral role in the Vietnam War. To give the Special Forces soldiers a symbol that would set them off from other members of the armed forces, Bank designed a unique hat, a green beret, as part of the uniform. The beret was at first met with hostility by Army commanders, who outlawed it. In 1961, President John F. Kennedy reinstated the beret and promised the men it would now be a permanent part of their uniform. "Wear the beret proudly," he told the men, "it will be a mark of distinction and a badge of courage in the difficult days ahead."

For Timothy McVeigh, just 22 years old, selection to serve in the Green Berets would be the realization of a dream. Since dropping out of college, McVeigh had drifted from job to job, searching for a purpose in life. During his idle hours, McVeigh found himself drawn to the gun culture—collecting firearms, reading gun magazines and going to trade shows where dealers sold guns. McVeigh didn't have much money in those days, but whenever he was able to scrape together a few dollars he would buy a gun. In the backyard of his father's home near Buffalo, New York, McVeigh set up a target range so he could practice shooting tin cans.

Still, McVeigh longed for direction in his life. In May 1988 a neighbor suggested to McVeigh that he consider the Army as a career. McVeigh thought it over and enlisted. After just a short time in the Army, McVeigh realized the best soldiers were Green Berets. He set his sights on selection for Special Forces.

But to be accepted into the Green Berets, McVeigh would have to undergo the Special Forces Assessment and Selection Program at Fort Bragg. It is a tough, three-week process of physical and mental tests designed to weed out all but the most promising soldiers. Indeed, about half of the candidates for Special Forces drop out during the assessment phase at Fort Bragg.

McVeigh was one of several Desert Storm veterans selected for the assessment program. But from the day of his arrival at Fort Bragg in early April 1991, it was clear that McVeigh and the other men who had served in the Gulf War were not ready for the rigorous examinations.

The first test required the candidates to do 52 push-ups in two minutes. McVeigh accomplished that goal easily, but had a bit of trouble with the next test—a 50-meter swim, in uniform and boots, in the Fort Bragg swimming pool. The test required McVeigh to swim two lengths of

the pool, but he quickly fell behind the other soldiers and was the last to finish. He had trouble kicking his legs; his water-logged boots felt as though they weighed a ton.

Next was the two-mile run. Again, McVeigh fell behind the other candidates and finished near the end of the pack.

The candidates headed to the Fort Bragg obstacle course where they would be required to climb trees, crawl under barbed wire, make their way through narrow tunnels, and wade across streams. This time, things went better for McVeigh. He passed many of the slower soldiers and finished the obstacle course in good time.

Still, by the end of the first day the commanders running the assessment program noticed that McVeigh wasn't the only candidate falling behind in many of the physical tests. Most of the Desert Storm veterans were having difficulty with the tests and it was clear why: after their experiences in the desert and their quick flights home, the men were simply exhausted. The commanders called the Gulf War soldiers together and asked if they wanted to

Soldiers wanting to join the elite fighting force called the Green Berets endure physical tests, including timed push-ups, swims and runs in full gear, and a lengthy obstacle course — and that's just the first day. The rigorous tests weed out unfit candidates.

drop out of the program, promising them that they would be given another chance to compete after they had had a few months to recuperate.

In the culture of the Green Berets, physical exhaustion is regarded as a poor excuse. Whenever a Special Forces soldier thinks he is too weary from work or a long march or lack of sleep to get the job done, he is supposed to reach deep inside himself and find the will to continue. McVeigh and the other Gulf War veterans were well aware of this attitude, and they feared that accepting the commanders' offer to drop out would be regarded as a sign of weakness. So consequently, the Gulf War veterans refused the offer. They would stick it out.

On the second day of the program, the candidates were told to prepare for a five-mile hike. The hike was to be made in full uniform and the candidates were instructed to carry rucksacks on their backs weighing 45 pounds. McVeigh threw some equipment in his rucksack, but after weighing it found the pack was about 20 pounds light. So he filled some plastic bags with sand and placed them in the pack.

The day was hot and muggy. The candidates marched through the woods, which offered cool shelter from the sun. During the hike, in the shade of the trees, McVeigh came to the realization that he was too exhausted to complete the rigorous selection program. By the time he arrived back at the barracks—again near the end of the pack—McVeigh had made the decision to drop out.

He filled out an Army form, a "Statement of Voluntary Withdrawal." On the statement, he was asked to write the reason for his withdrawal. McVeigh wrote: "The rucksack march hurt more than it should. I just can't hack it."

McVeigh returned to Fort Riley in Kansas, where his Bradley Fighting Vehicle unit was based. Over the next several months, the sergeant lost interest in an Army career. He began spending long periods in the barracks, rarely taking advantage of weekend leave. Instead, he resumed his hobby of collecting guns, hiding them in his Army footlocker—a violation of the service's rules. He started going to gun shows in Kansas, even becoming a gun dealer himself. Next, he moved off the Fort Riley base, renting a house in nearby Herington, Kansas, with two other soldiers—Sergeant Rick Cerney and Corporal John Kelso. The three men didn't get along. Kelso found McVeigh was developing racist ideas. It was clear to Kelso that McVeigh didn't like African Americans. McVeigh talked to his housemates about the "survivalist" culture—people who believe it is important to arm themselves for a future breakdown of law and order in America. Kelso also found himself afraid to ride in a car with McVeigh.

"He drove very, very fast," Kelso said. "No conscience for laws at all."

Within a month, McVeigh found another house off base—this time with Sergeant Royal Witcher. In this case, McVeigh got along with his housemate—the two men became close friends—but even Witcher admitted that McVeigh made him nervous at times. McVeigh kept guns all over the house, even in the bathroom. Witcher also noticed that McVeigh never left the house unarmed, always keeping numerous guns in his car. Indeed, the arsenal in McVeigh's trunk included shotguns, pistols, rifles, and even a machine gun McVeigh obtained from a manufacturer in the Czech Republic.

"Why do you always carry a gun?" Witcher asked McVeigh.

"You never know," McVeigh answered.

Some of his ideas and habits seemed even more outlandish. McVeigh told friends that he believed the Army planted a computer chip in his buttocks as a way to

At Fort Riley, Kansas, Timothy McVeigh trained with his Bradley Fighting Unit squad and received high awards. Some soldiers who lived with McVeigh said his racist and anarchist attitudes made them uncomfortable.

monitor his activities. In the house he shared with Witcher, McVeigh maintained a Spartan existence. His bedroom contained few furnishings, and for a curtain he hung an Army poncho over the window. He read *The Turner Diaries,* a novel that told of a racist regime that takes over the government following a nuclear holocaust. McVeigh became a believer in the book's antigovernment message and urged his friends to read the book. In the early mornings, McVeigh would often traipse out to the Fort Riley rifle range by himself where he could shoot guns in solitude.

Back at Fort Riley, McVeigh seemed for a time to be as dedicated a soldier as he had been in the Persian Gulf. He earned high marks for his work on the Bradley Fighting Vehicle and even received an offer to join the staff of the battalion commander. Joining the commander's staff was regarded as an honor, but McVeigh knew his responsibilities as an aide to the commander meant a change from gunner to desk sergeant. McVeigh enjoyed his duty aboard the Bradley, mostly because he enjoyed firing the tank's heavy guns. He had no taste for desk work.

So when he was summoned to the commander's office, McVeigh told his boss that he had no interest in signing on as a member of his staff. In fact, McVeigh said, he had decided to leave the Army.

The commander was shocked. He asked McVeigh for his reason.

"I, I just feel I need to leave," McVeigh said.

He left the Army in December 1991, after serving nearly four years. He had earned numerous medals and commendations for his service in the Persian Gulf. Nevertheless, McVeigh had soured on Army life. He had failed the test for Special Forces, which meant he would never serve in the military's most elite unit. And as McVeigh became more immersed in the gun and survivalist cultures, he found himself questioning the role of government in people's lives. As a member of the armed forces, McVeigh was an agent of the federal government, sworn to uphold its laws, and defend America against its enemies.

For someone who had come to believe that his real enemy was the government of America, a career in the Army was unthinkable.

"Tim was the perfect soldier. I swear to God he could have been sergeant major of the Army," recalled Robin Littleton, one of McVeigh's closest friends in the Army. "Before this, I'd never heard Tim talk bad about the military. I think he felt he got a raw deal, and he wanted out."

Shortly after leaving the Army, McVeigh sent Littleton a letter. On the letter, McVeigh had drawn a pistol and skull and crossbones.

The letter ominously said: "So many victims, so little time."

A Mass
Casualty
Incident

The blast that tore open the Alfred P. Murrah Building rocked buildings for miles, some so significantly that people inside ran for cover. Pedestrians on the street had to dodge tons of flying debris.

J ust a few minutes before nine o'clock on the morning of April 19, 1995, Edye Smith dropped off her two young sons at the day-care center in the Alfred P. Murrah Federal Building in Oklahoma City, Oklahoma.

Her sons, Chase, aged three, and Colton, aged two, were still eating their doughnuts when Smith walked them through the doors of the day-care center on the second floor of the building. She kissed the boys on the cheeks, then wiped the powdered sugar from their doughnuts off her lips.

As she turned to walk away, Colton called out to her. "I love you, Mommy," he said.

Smith stopped to embrace her children one final time, then left the

Chase Dalton Smith, only three years old, and his younger brother Colton, died in the Oklahoma City bombing. Seventeen other children also attending day care in the Murrah building died that day.

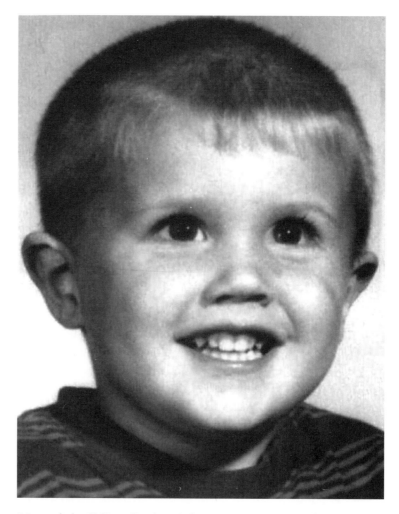

Murrah building for her job as a secretary at the Internal Revenue Service five blocks away.

As Edye Smith arrived at her desk, Richard E. Williams was already at work in his office in the Murrah building. Williams was the assistant building manager for the General Services Administration, the federal agency that maintains the government's buildings. It was Williams' job to oversee the operation of the Murrah building itself, making sure the heating and air-conditioning systems as well as the elevators, bathrooms, and other building services ran in proper order.

The building had been named in honor of a federal judge from Oklahoma who died in 1970. Williams, 50, had worked in the Murrah building since it opened in 1977, joining the General Services Administration staff as a maintenance mechanic. His office was on the first floor, just 100 feet from the building's entrance. He knew almost everybody who worked in the Murrah building.

By 9 A.M., Susan Gail Hunt had already been at work for more than an hour. She worked as a supervisor in the office of the department of Housing and Urban Development (H.U.D.) on the eighth floor of the Murrah building. H.U.D. is the federal agency that oversees housing programs for impoverished Americans. At 9 o'clock, Hunt stopped at Kim Clark's desk. Clark and Hunt were friends; Clark was planning to get married soon, and Hunt had agreed to arrange the wedding bouquets.

"Do you have the flowers yet?" Clark asked.

"This weekend," Hunt assured her friend.

Michael Norfleet arrived at the Murrah building a few minutes before 9 o'clock, and was delighted to find a parking space on Fifth Street directly in front of the building. Norfleet put some coins in the parking meter, noticing that he had parked in front of a Ryder rental truck.

Norfleet was an officer in the Marine Corps. He didn't work in the building, but decided to stop off in the Marine Corps recruiting office on the sixth floor to see if a friend, Benjamin Davis, had won a promotion. Norfleet found Davis already in the recruiting office. Norfleet made a call to check on the promotion, but the line was busy. He decided to stretch his legs, promising Davis he'd return in a few minutes to place the call again.

As he walked across the recruiting office, Norfleet found himself thinking about the Ryder truck he had seen just a few minutes before. Norfleet thought it was unusual to see the truck parked out front; usually, trucks making deliveries to the Murrah building would pull around back to the loading dock. Then, he saw two sergeants he knew and approached them to say hello.

"Just about the time I got hello and good morning out of my mouth," Norfleet recalled, "the bomb hit."

A massive explosion rocked the Murrah building at 9:02 A.M., disintegrating the front of the towering edifice. Tons of concrete, steel, and other debris came crashing down, sending shock waves reverberating for miles throughout Oklahoma City. Glass from the building's windows became flying missiles, shooting out in all directions, striking and injuring unprotected pedestrians on the streets below. Seconds after the blast, a witness working in a nearby building recalled seeing paper floating gently to the street. The blast had ruptured filing cabinets inside the building and shot their contents— hundreds of thousands of documents—into the breezy Oklahoma City morning.

Across the street, Trent Smith was lying in bed in the Oklahoma City YMCA when the shock from the bombing lifted him seven feet in the air and tossed him toward the window. At 240 pounds, Smith was a big man, but his body was tossed about as though it were a feather. Suddenly, Smith found himself hanging halfway out the square hole that had once been the window. He crawled back into his room, realizing how near death he had been. As he shook himself back to consciousness, Smith heard a man screaming down the hall. "He said he couldn't walk," Smith recalled, "but I told him that you gotta get out of there because there might be another bomb. You gotta get out!"

Just down the street from the Murrah building, Cynthia Lou Klaver had just convened a meeting of the Oklahoma Water Resources Board, an agency that decides how the state distributes water. As a prairie state,

Oklahoma is often hit with drought conditions, and the Water Resources Board was established to make sure water is not wasted. Klaver, a lawyer, had opened a hearing into a farmer's request to withdraw groundwater from his land for a bottled-water business. Klaver was in the habit of tape recording the meetings. She had just turned on the tape deck when the blast hit the Murrah building; the shock waves were so strong that Klaver and the others thought their building had been struck by the explosion as well. Klaver's voice was caught on the Water Resources Board tape deck.

"Everybody get out . . . out!" she shouted. "Watch the electricity lines. Watch the lines! Out the back door. All the way to the right . . . Let's get out of here . . . ."

The 168 people who died in the bombing and the many who survived had just arrived at the Murrah Building. They attended to day-to-day business on the building's nine floors as the Ryder truck parked outside exploded.

Jon Hansen felt and heard the blast, too. Hansen was an assistant fire chief for Oklahoma City, on duty in his firehouse several blocks away.

"To the east, the sky was full of dust and dense black smoke," Hansen said. "You couldn't see anything through it—that's how thick it was. It darkened the streets, covering at least a square block. We scrambled to our vehicles and headed east down Fifth Street."

At the Murrah building, what Hansen and the other emergency workers discovered was death, misery, and complete chaos. They quickly waded into the rubble in an effort to find people still alive beneath the tons of debris.

"It was instantly clear to all of us that we were in the middle of a major incident," Hansen said. "For a moment I just stood there, stunned by what I was seeing. The entire front of this huge building was gone. My mind raced ahead, wondering about the fate of the hundreds of people inside. I knew we had what we refer to in our business as a 'mass casualty incident.' As I made my way to the front of the federal building, which faces north, I saw toys lying among the debris in the street. And it hit me. There was a day-care center inside. My heart sank."

Across the country, in Washington D.C., President Bill Clinton was meeting in the White House with Tansu Ciller, the prime minister of Turkey. The issue Clinton and Ciller were discussing at that moment was Turkey's attack on Kurdish rebels in northern Iraq, which Ciller told the president was authorized in order to combat terrorism in her own country. A White House aide rushed into the room, leaned over, and told Clinton the CNN television network had just reported that an explosion leveled a federal building in Oklahoma City. Clinton told the aide to find out what he could.

Minutes later, another aide slipped the president a

Rescue workers sift through the rubble five days after the bombing. The rescue effort went on for weeks. Although rescue workers saved many lives, the death toll climbed to 168 people.

note. It read: "Half of federal building in Oklahoma City blown up—expect heavy casualties."

The death toll would eventually reach 168 people—including 19 children in the day-care center.

■   ■   ■

While rescue workers sifted feverishly through the rubble in search of victims, many people at the scene began to wonder about the cause of the blast. More and more, it didn't seem likely that the catastrophe was the result of an accident such as a gas line explosion, an earthquake, or a structural defect in the building itself. In this case, the destruction had the look and feel of terrorism.

As the name suggests, terrorists attempt to terrorize, or strike fear, into a society or group of people by threatening or committing acts of violence. Indeed, they desire their actions to be public displays of violence so their message is heard and understood by as many people as possible. In the end, they hope to achieve political goals, such as changing conditions in society or even overthrowing a government.

Terrorists are frequently members of groups, although they usually act alone or in small squads known as "cells." The identities of their leaders and members are often kept secret, making it difficult for law enforcement agencies to track them down or defeat the larger group. While the individual terrorist or terrorist cell may be captured or killed, the organization remains intact and authorities can only guess at its precise structure and membership.

Terrorists may target governments, political parties, ethnic or religious groups, corporations, or members of the news media. Sometimes they carry out political assassinations, but most often the violence is directed at random victims—passengers on a bus or airplane, for example, or young people dancing in a nightclub or shopping at a mall. The randomness of the attack serves an important terrorist goal: bringing fear to, and undermining the sense of security of, large numbers of people. Simply by virtue of their being in the wrong place at the wrong time, they too could be victims. Many terrorists are willing to give their own lives for the cause, acting as suicide bombers with the belief that their deeds will bring about change. Indeed, terrorism is more about sending a message than making victims suffer. That is why terrorist groups are quick to claim responsibility for their crimes and welcome press interest in their activities.

In many areas of the world, terrorism seems to be a way of life. In the Middle East, Palestinians fighting for a homeland have committed hundreds of terrorist acts against the government and people of Israel. Occasionally, Israelis have struck back with terrorist acts themselves.

But terrorism is not a practice limited to the Middle East. Over the years, even Americans have suffered at the hands of terrorists. In the early part of the 20th Century, the anarchist movement grew strong in America. Its leaders advocated a violent overthrow of the government so that a socialist society could be installed in the United States, similar to how the Bolsheviks seized power in Russia to form the Soviet Union. In 1920, 38 people were killed on Wall Street in New York City when an anarchist's bomb exploded during lunchtime in the city's financial district.

In the 1950s, terrorists advocating an independent Puerto Rico attempted to assassinate President Harry Truman. The attempt was unsuccessful, but in 1975 four people were killed when a bomb planted by Puerto Rican separatists exploded in historic Fraunces Tavern in New York City.

In 1993, fundamentalist Arabs attempted to blow up the World Trade Center in New York City. The bomb, which had been set off in the building's garage, killed six people and caused millions of dollars in damage. Although the truck carrying the bomb was blown to bits, investigators were able to find the vehicle identification number on the chassis, which led them to the terrorist who had rented the vehicle three days before the bombing. That lead enabled authorities to track down 26 members of the ring.

But the 1993 attack on the World Trade Center offered just a slight hint of the horror that was to come. In 2001, fanatical Arab terrorists hijacked two commercial airliners and flew them into the twin towers of the World Trade Center, destroying the buildings, and killing and injuring more than 3,000 people. On the same morning, a third plane crashed into the Pentagon, headquarters of the American military in Washington D.C., while a fourth plane plummeted into a wooded area near Pittsburgh, Pennsylvania. It, too, had been hijacked and was apparently heading for a target in Washington D.C. when it crashed. Investigators believe the plane crashed when passengers rushed the terrorists in a heroic but ill-fated effort to take back control of the plane.

■   ■   ■

Richard Williams was knocked over by hundreds of pieces of concrete, glass, and metal that shot by his body in the seconds following the bombing of the Murrah building. Williams collapsed unconscious into the debris. Minutes later, he shook himself awake, discovering that he was buried under the rubble. And yet, he heard a faint voice that said: "Hang on. I'll be right back."

The voice belonged to Terry Yeakey, an Oklahoma City policeman. Yeakey had seen Williams' arm hanging out of the rubble. Yeakey dug Williams out of the debris, then carried him away from the building on his back.

Williams suffered a broken arm. Also, an ear had nearly been severed from his head. But he was alive.

Susan Gail Hunt survived the blast as well. But Kim Clark, whose wedding Hunt was helping to plan, was killed by the explosion. So were 10 more of Hunt's coworkers in the HUD office.

Michael Norfleet survived the explosion as well, but Benjamin Davis never found out whether he received his promotion. He was killed by the bombing.

Cynthia Lou Klaver and the others attending the

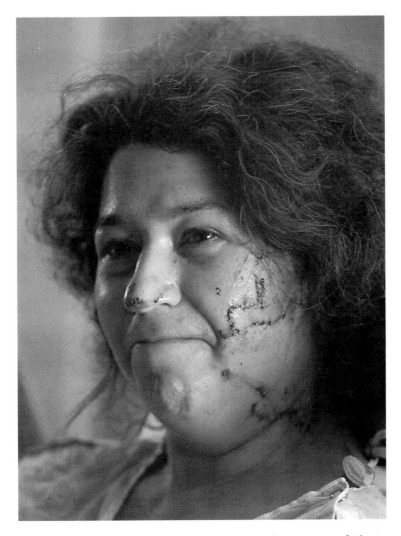

Susan Urbach, injured in the bombing, worked across the street from the Murrah Building. Doctors used 200 stitches to close up her wounds.

Water Resources Board hearing made it out of their building alive.

"I thought the whole building was coming down on us," she said. "I didn't see any way we were going to make it out. The building shook and the whole ceiling fell down. And lights continued to fall even after the original cave-in. There was debris, lights, wires, lines hanging down all over. Electricity was still running, so the lights were on, and everyone was bewildered."

It took days to find survivors. Units from the U.S. Air

Force and National Guard soon arrived to help dig through the debris. Sixty firefighters from Arizona trained in finding victims in collapsed buildings were called in. Cranes and backhoes were driven onto the site to remove the rubble.

Special listening devices helped detect sounds of life beneath the rock and steel. Dogs were also led into the rescue area to sniff for signs of life. Those activities were necessary, but they actually slowed down the rescue work. Whenever someone thought they heard sounds made by a survivor, all of the heavy equipment on the site had to be shut down so the listening devices could be operated.

The rescue teams worked throughout the day, and when night fell they set up blazing spotlights so they could work at night as well. The rescue workers used heavy equipment, shovels, pickaxes, and their bare hands. Sometimes, they could move no more than an inch or two of rubble at a time. Occasionally, they were able to locate a victim.

Rescue workers found Dana Bradley in the Murrah building's basement, trapped under the rubble of cement girders. By the time they reached her, the 20-year-old woman had lost a lot of blood. As firemen tried to free her, the building shook and they were forced to evacuate—leaving the terrified woman behind. They returned a few minutes later, accompanied by a doctor. After working for a few more minutes, the firemen determined that Bradley's leg was crushed under twisted shards of rebar—the steel used to reinforce concrete in large buildings—and that to save her life the doctor would have to amputate her leg.

Bradley begged them not to do it, but they had no choice. What's more, the doctor could administer little anesthesia. Bradley had lost so much blood that the doctor feared too much painkiller would send her into a coma. So the surgeon went to work, and while Bradley screamed in pain, he amputated her leg below the knee.

The firemen pulled her out and carried her quickly out of the basement to a waiting ambulance. Dana Bradley survived the ordeal, but she lost her mother and two children in the blast.

When Edye Smith arrived at her office at the Internal Revenue Service (I.R.S.), she discovered her coworkers had planned a surprise birthday party for her. Edye would be turning 23 years old later that week. The I.R.S. employees gave Edye a cake, and as she stood to slice the cake she heard the explosion. Everyone rushed to the office windows and saw smoke rising from the vicinity of the Murrah building.

"I turned to a coworker and said 'That's so sad. That's some little child's mother that's been killed,'" Smith recalled.

Smith and her coworkers made their way out of the I.R.S. building down to the street below where Smith met her mother, Kathy Graham-Wilburn, who also worked for the I.R.S. Smith and Graham-Wilburn approached the bombing site, and soon realized the Murrah building was at ground zero.

The two women knifed their way through the crowd, rushing from child to child, examining each sobbing face, slowly coming to the numbing realization that Chase and Colton Smith were not among the survivors.

■   ■   ■

Just before 10:30 A.M. on the morning of the explosion, Timothy McVeigh was driving north on Interstate 35 in Oklahoma when he noticed he was being followed by an Oklahoma Highway Patrol car. McVeigh was at the wheel of an old Mercury Marquis. The vehicle caught the state trooper's attention because it didn't have a license plate.

Soon, the patrol car came alongside the Mercury and the trooper signaled McVeigh to pull over. McVeigh nodded, and slowed his car to a stop along the shoulder of the road. McVeigh had been stopped just outside of Perry, Oklahoma, about 60 miles north of Oklahoma City.

McVeigh knew the trooper stopped him because the Mercury had no license plate. He had removed the plate four days earlier when he parked the car in downtown Oklahoma City, a few blocks from the Murrah building. McVeigh took the plate off the car to discourage car thieves from stealing the parked vehicle.

The state trooper's name was Charles J. Hanger, a 19-year veteran of the Oklahoma Highway Patrol. Hanger parked the patrol car behind the Mercury and slowly approached the vehicle.

Most people remain in their cars when they are stopped by a policeman, so Hanger was surprised when the tall man in the Mercury stepped out of the car to face him. Hanger was wary. He knew about the bombing at the Murrah building because he had originally been summoned to Oklahoma City, then told to turn back because enough police were already on hand at the blast site. But also, two weeks before, another state trooper made a traffic stop near Perry and the motorist responded by drawing a gun. Shots were exchanged and the motorist was wounded.

Hanger asked McVeigh to produce his driver's license. As McVeigh reached around to his back pocket to retrieve his wallet, Hanger noticed a bulge under McVeigh's jacket.

"What's that?" the trooper asked.

"I have a gun," McVeigh said.

Slowly, Hanger extended his hand and felt the hard metal beneath McVeigh's jacket. Quickly, the trooper drew his own gun and pointed it at McVeigh's face.

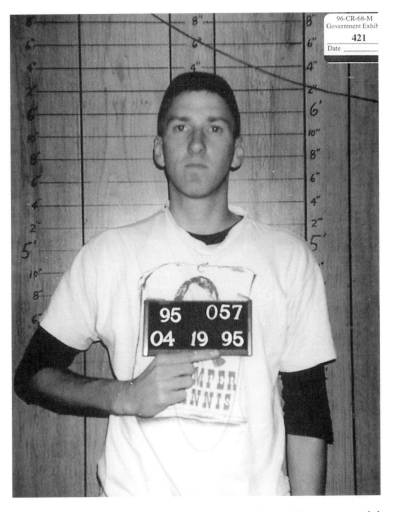

96-CR-68-M
Government Exhib

421

Date _____

Timothy McVeigh's mug shot after an officer took him into custody on firearm charges. The officer stopped McVeigh on an interstate highway outside Oklahoma City just hours after the blast.

"Move your hands away, slowly," Hanger told McVeigh. "Get both hands up in the air."

McVeigh showed no resistance. He placed his hands against the trunk of the Mercury and spread his feet, allowing the trooper to search his body. Hanger took the gun away from McVeigh as well as an ammunition clip and a knife. Next, he put handcuffs on McVeigh.

"You know," he told McVeigh, "when you carry a gun around like that, one wrong move could get you shot."

McVeigh said he realized that was possible.

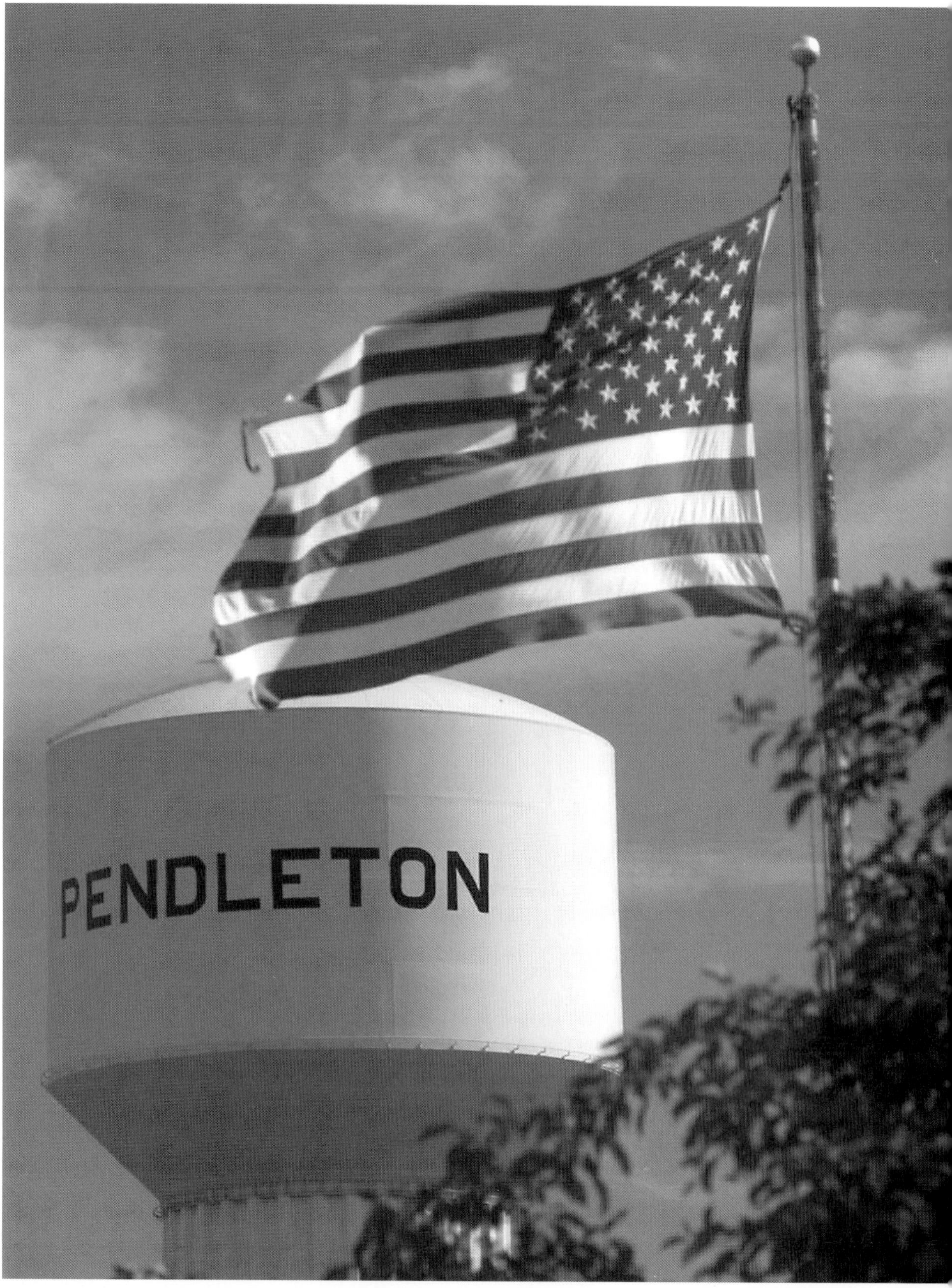
PENDLETON

Billy the Kid

When Timothy McVeigh was nine years old, a blizzard swept
through western New York State that dumped record
amounts of snowfall on the city of Buffalo and nearby
communities. The storm paralyzed the region. Streets were buried under
tons of snow, mail delivery and mass transit were halted, and people were
unable to venture far from their homes.

Of course, for most kids in the Buffalo area it was heaven on Earth. Schools
closed for nearly three weeks, leaving children time for freedom and adventure
in the mountains of snow that were left behind by the storm. McVeigh and his
friends in Pendleton, New York, were out every day, tunneling into the piles
of snow created by the plows. One day, the boys dug down into a pile of snow
and gleefully found the roof of a car that had been buried by the plow.

Timothy McVeigh led a normal, unremarkable child-hood. He was born in 1968, the son of Bill and Mildred McVeigh. His father was a factory worker at a plant that made car radiators; his mother, whom everybody called Mickey, was a travel agent. The couple had two other children: Patty, who was two years older than Tim, and Jennifer, six years younger.

When Tim was seven years old, his grandfather, Ed McVeigh, planted the seeds for the boy's lifelong fascina-tion with guns when he taught him how to shoot a rifle. Ed McVeigh would often take the boy target shooting along the nearby Erie Canal, where he would set up empty cans in a wooded ravine, allowing Tim to hone his aim by firing off rounds at the cans. Later, in the Army, McVeigh earned the status of an expert marksman and won several commendations for his sure aim.

Bill and Mickey were devoted to their children, but there were problems in the marriage. When Tim was in high school, his mother moved out of the house and eventu-ally filed for divorce. Tim chose to remain with his father, seeing his mother mostly when he dropped by her office in town. In school, Tim was regarded as intelligent but there was no question that he was an underachiever. He won a small scholarship to college, but lasted just a few months at Bryant and Stratton Business College, a school near Pendle-ton. He had been planning a career as a computer program-mer but quickly grew bored with the classes. Instead of reading the books that had been assigned by his professors, McVeigh found himself interested more in gun magazines, such as *Guns & Ammo.* He also read a book titled *To Ride, Shoot and Speak the Truth,* written by Jeff Cooper, an expert on handguns. The book was a tactical guide on how to use handguns in warfare but it talked about much more, includ-ing the importance of defending oneself and one's honor, and even discussed the likelihood of nuclear war. As for

McVeigh's taste in movies, he was fascinated with stories of survival—*Red Dawn,* in which high school students resist a Russian invasion of America was a favorite movie. He also liked *Logan's Run,* in which a rebel flees police in a futuristic totalitarian society, and the original *Planet of the Apes* movies, which featured humans making a stand against simian conquerors in a world decimated by nuclear holocaust.

His interests now straying far from computer programming, McVeigh dropped out of college and found a job at a Burger King.

In his spare time, McVeigh visited gun stores in Pendleton and nearby Lockport and bought guns himself whenever he had the money. At the stores, McVeigh always found gun enthusiasts willing to talk about

Timothy McVeigh frequented gun shows near his hometown. At the gun shows, activists intent on halting gun control laws influenced McVeigh's attitude about the government. The activists claimed that such laws revoked a citizen's Second Amendment right to bear arms.

weapons and the laws governing their use. Clearly, McVeigh learned, gun owners were not happy about current trends in the law—they believed many federal and state legislators seemed intent on finding ways to rein in people's Second Amendment rights. At the stores, he also found pamphlets from local organizations warning gun owners that the government was willing to go to any length to take the guns out of their hands. One pamphlet he found was published by the local chapter of the Shooters Committee for Political Education, known as S.C.O.P.E. The pamphlet said: "Our fight is really about LIBERTY and FREEDOM! We must be ever vigilant to protect our liberty, for there are those whose goal is to steal it from us."

■   ■   ■

In March 1981, when Timothy McVeigh was 13 years old, a mentally troubled young man named John Hinckley Jr. stood outside the Hilton Hotel in Washington D.C., waiting for President Ronald Reagan to conclude a speech. As Reagan walked out of the hotel toward a waiting limousine, Hinckley emerged from the crowd of onlookers, drew a handgun, and fired at the president.

Hinckley's shots struck Reagan in the ribs; although wounded, the president recovered and was able to serve eight years in office. Three other men were wounded in the attack, including a Washington D.C. policeman, a Secret Service agent and the president's press secretary, James Brady. All three men survived the assault, but Brady's wound proved to be the most serious. Struck in the head by one of Hinckley's shots, Brady never fully recovered his motor or cognitive skills. Years after the attack, Brady's speech is slurred and he has remained confined to a wheelchair.

But what John Hinckley failed to destroy in Jim Brady and his wife Sarah was their resolve to take guns out of the hands of criminals and mentally deranged people like Hinckley. Gun control advocates rallied around the Bradys, and soon there was a national call for Congress to adopt the "Brady Bill," a tough measure that would force people seeking to buy guns to undergo investigations by police into their backgrounds before they could obtain the weapons. Many gun owners seethed at the provisions of the proposed law. They saw no reason why government should be granted permission to look into their private lives, and viewed any effort to regulate the sale of guns as a clear violation of their Second Amendment rights.

The Second Amendment is one of the 10 original amendments to the U.S. Constitution known as the "Bill of Rights." The Constitution that was adopted by the 13 original states following the American Revolution established a government but did not speak to the rights of the citizens. And so, the nation's founding fathers soon got down to work to draft a set of laws that would ensure the rights that had often been denied people by the monarchs of European nations. In 1791, the Bill of Rights was ratified by the states and it became part of the Constitution.

Among the rights guaranteed by the first 10 amendments are the right of Americans to worship as they please, the right of the press to act independently of the government, the freedom of people to speak publicly and to petition the government for change, and the rights of defendants to receive fair, public, and speedy trials.

For gun owners, the Second Amendment held the most significance.

It reads: "A well-regulated militia, being necessary to the security of a free State, the right of the people to keep and bear arms, shall not be infringed."

Although the right to bear arms was now guaranteed by the Constitution, state and local governments felt they had to take steps to regulate the use of firearms. Over the years, a smorgasbord of different laws regulating how guns could be used and carried was adopted by states and cities depending on the mood of local lawmakers and the desires of their constituents. In big cities where urban crime is an issue, such as New York City, lawmakers passed strict gun laws that required people to receive permits from the government before they could legally obtain and carry guns. In some of the western states, such as Texas, few gun laws were passed and people enjoyed wide-ranging freedom to own and carry firearms.

The federal government passed major gun control laws in 1934 and 1938, establishing taxes on gun sales, barring convicted felons from owning guns and requiring gun dealers and manufacturers to obtain licenses. Three decades later, in response to the assassinations of Senator Robert F. Kennedy and the Reverend Martin Luther King Jr., Congress passed the Gun Control Act of 1968, which banned interstate commerce of guns by unlicensed dealers, required manufacturers to engrave guns with serial numbers, banned the import of cheap handguns known as "Saturday Night Specials," and set the minimum age for handgun purchases at 21 and long guns at 18. The Bureau of Alcohol, Tobacco and Firearms was given authority to enforce those laws.

Following the attempt on President Reagan's life, the Bradys became tireless crusaders for an additional federal gun control law that would require police background checks on all gun purchasers as well as a "cooling-off" period of three days before the customer could take the weapon home. Progress on the federal level was slow, mostly because of the influence of the National Rifle Association—an organization of gun owners who count

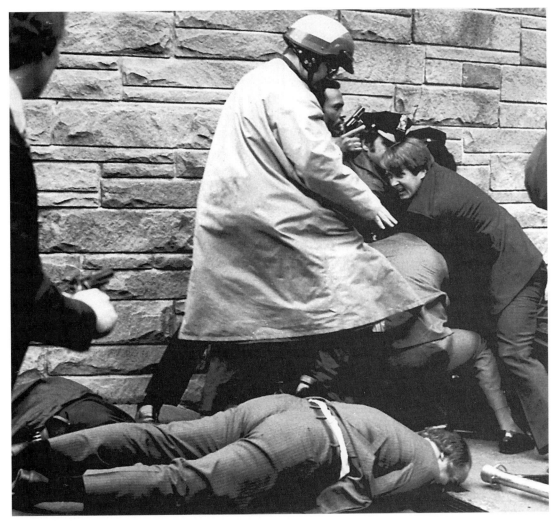

many conservative members of Congress on their side. But in several of the states, legislatures responded by independently toughening their gun control laws.

In 1989, California banned private ownership of semiautomatic assault weapons. That same year, Florida passed a law requiring gun owners to keep their weapons under lock. Virginia would soon become the first state to pass legislation limiting people to buying one gun per month.

In 1993, after years of resistance organized by the

James Brady lies on the sidewalk wounded by a bullet intended for then-President Ronald Reagan. Brady's injury in 1980 fueled a federal campaign against concealed weapons that resulted in a law requiring a waiting period and background check for all potential gun buyers.

National Rifle Association, Congress finally passed what became known as the Brady Law. The measure was signed into law by President Bill Clinton. Now, everybody who wanted to buy a gun in America would have to undergo a background check by police and endure the cooling-off period.

And Congress wasn't finished. A year later, Clinton signed the federal Violent Crime and Control Act of 1994, banning the manufacture and future private ownership of military-style assault weapons.

Many gun owners looked at the developments on the federal level and saw their rights quickly eroding. Indeed, one of those gun owners who bristled at the government's efforts to tread on his rights was Timothy McVeigh.

■   ■   ■

McVeigh wasn't satisfied with his job at the Burger King. The salary was low, he was bored, and he ached to find more meaningful employment. The idea of becoming a security guard intrigued him. It would, after all, permit him to carry a gun while on duty. In 1987, he found a job with the Burke Armored Car service in Buffalo. McVeigh's job was to guard cash shipments heading for businesses and banks in Buffalo. He relished the job and was a model employee. One of the company's duties was to send an armored car to the airport to meet shipments of millions of dollars in cash bound for the Federal Reserve Bank in Buffalo. McVeigh was often called on to provide security for the shipment. Still not yet 20 years old, McVeigh had turned into one of Burke's most trusted workers. His coworkers called him "Billy the Kid" because of his boyish looks, his enthusiasm for the job, and his reputation as the best marksman on the staff.

McVeigh found himself guarding cash shipments as

his armored truck drove through African-American neighborhoods in Buffalo. In Pendleton, McVeigh had rarely seen a black face. Now, for the first time, he was seeing inner-city culture and society up close. As the armored car drove by the tenements and burned-out buildings in Buffalo's most distressed neighborhoods, McVeigh would listen as the older Burke employees complained about blacks, accusing them of living off welfare payments, which they regarded as government handouts. Slowly, McVeigh adopted their racist attitudes.

Back home in Pendleton, McVeigh was still intrigued by the survivalist culture. Survivalists believe a break-down in society is imminent, and they must stockpile food, water, tools—and especially guns—in order to survive when the holocaust arrives. McVeigh did just that, stocking up supplies and storing them in his father's basement.

One day, Bill McVeigh was surprised when a delivery truck dropped off two large 55-gallon drums that had been ordered by his son. Bill McVeigh, who never spent much time in his basement, began to look around down there, and soon discovered that his son was prepared for the worst.

"That's when I realized he had this cabinet, and he had all this stuff," Bill McVeigh said. "He had gun-powder in there, whatever he thought he needed. If everything went haywire, he'd have it there. You know, he was into survival."

Bill McVeigh asked his son what the drums were for.

"Water," Tim answered. "If we need it."

McVeigh spent virtually his entire salary on expensive guns. The problem was he had no place to shoot them. That issue was solved when McVeigh and Dave Darlak, a high school buddy, scraped together $400 for a down payment on 10 acres of scrubland in the backwoods near

Survivalists believe society will eventually break down and they must prepare to survive. Timothy McVeigh used a piece of land he owned to practice survivalist drills and shoot guns.

Olean, New York. Darlak hardly used the property, but McVeigh spent many happy hours there, firing rounds from a variety of guns. In fact, he went there every weekend, even camping overnight. McVeigh would dress in camouflage gear, scampering around the terrain, practicing the tactics he had read about in the survivalist literature. Occasionally, some local farmers would complain about the noise, they claimed it was scaring their chickens, but for the most part McVeigh could fire off his guns in solitude.

McVeigh told his coworkers at Burke about the target range. His supervisor at Burke, Vincent Capparra, said: "He was a survivalist. That's what he told us. He said if they ever blew up a bomb or anything, you know, if we ever were bombed, he would have a place he could put his stuff and be safe."

Although he enjoyed his job as a security guard and freedom to shoot guns at his private target range, McVeigh still found himself wandering aimlessly through life. In early 1988, Darlak told McVeigh he was planning to join the Army. Then, Richard Drzyzga, a neighbor, suggested McVeigh do the same.

"Tim, you've got to do something with your life," Drzyzga told him. "You've got to focus. Why don't you join the service, get into the military? It's a perfect solution for you. You like weapons. They can give you all the weapons you want. And you can learn something besides, and maybe you can bring something home and be useful."

On May 24, 1988, Timothy McVeigh walked into an Army recruiting office in Buffalo and enlisted. Four days later, he arrived at Fort Benning in Georgia for basic training. That night, he became friendly with another recruit who bunked next to him in the barracks.

The other recruit's name was Terry Lynn Nichols.

FORT BENNING GA
ECHO   4TH-36TH
INFANTRY REGIMENT
    2   PLATOON
   WILD DEUCE
3 JUNE   1988

Timothy McVeigh met Terry Nichols while stationed at the U.S. Army base at Fort Benning, Georgia. The two pose here with their platoon. McVeigh is third from the right in the back row. Nichols is at the left end of the front row.

Patriots

4

Terry Nichols and Timothy McVeigh became inseparable in the Army. Their backgrounds were similar—both men grew up in broken homes and both had dropped out of college. They both collected guns and were ardent believers in Second Amendment rights. They shared other beliefs as well. Back home, McVeigh was a survivalist. Nichols was no survivalist, but he didn't trust the government and, like McVeigh, expected the social order to break down.

In fact, Nichols harbored a deep resentment toward the government and blamed it for many of the things that had gone wrong in his life. At 33, Nichols had chosen an Army career relatively late in life, he was much older than the other recruits who were barely older than high school kids. But he had failed in a number of businesses, the last of which was farming. When he lost his Michigan farm in a court case, Nichols fumed that the government had a hand in his farm's demise. With no job and no money, Nichols joined the Army. He walked into an Army recruiting office in Michigan the same day McVeigh enlisted in Buffalo.

Nichols and McVeigh both impressed their commanders. Nichols, partly because of his age, was regarded as a natural leader whom the other recruits looked up to; the company's commanders responded by appointing him as senior platoon leader. As for McVeigh, he was an eager soldier. He pushed his body to the limits of physical endurance in Fort Benning's tough basic training program, setting an example that the other new soldiers found themselves following. Company commanders recognized McVeigh's influence on the others, and named him leader of one of his platoon's six-man squads.

"Two days into training, Tim and Terry were like brothers," said William Dilly. "They were drawn to each other. It was almost like Tim idolized Terry."

McVeigh and Nichols shared ideas about race as well. Back in Pendleton, McVeigh knew few African Americans and grew into a racist as he rode through black neighborhoods in the Burke armored cars. Nichols, who grew up on a farm, had never been exposed to inner-city blacks in his youth, either. By the time he joined the Army, he harbored a resentment toward blacks as well.

"If you said anything about welfare or any government entitlements or anything like that, you'd hear an hour speech from either of them," Dilly said.

Basic training ended after three months. McVeigh and Nichols headed to Fort Riley in Kansas, where they joined a battalion in the First Infantry Division—the Army's famed "Big Red One," which had fought together since World War I. They were joined by a third soldier

from Fort Benning with whom they became friendly—
Michael J. Fortier, an Arizona native who also harbored
antigovernment political views.

The three men were tight. They were members of the
same squad, and enjoyed spending time together on the
Fort Riley rifle range where they could fire their
weapons. Nichols found a farmer off base who let them
use his land to target shoot in their leisure hours as well.
Fortier was unlike Nichols and McVeigh in one regard,
though: he was a heavy drinker and marijuana user,
and he took other drugs as well. McVeigh and Nichols
tolerated their friend's substance abuse.

In the spring of 1989, Nichols shocked his two friends
when he sought an emergency discharge from the Army.
Nichols, who left a family back in Michigan when he
joined up, had to return because his wife Lana was
having trouble supporting herself and the couple's 10-
year-old son Josh.

Just before leaving the Army, Nichols pulled aside
Glen Edwards, a fellow battalion member, and told him
that he planned to return to Fort Riley one day in search
of recruits for a new type of army—one that wouldn't
necessarily fight to protect the United States government.
He asked Edwards to join up when the time came.

"He told me he would come back to Fort Riley to start
his own military organization," Edwards said. "He said
he could get any kind of weapon and any equipment he
wanted. I can't remember the name of his organization,
but he seemed pretty serious about it."

Nichols also told Edwards that Fortier and McVeigh
were willing recruits for the organization. Certainly, in
McVeigh's case, that was no exaggeration. While at Fort
Riley, McVeigh had discovered a book titled *The Turner
Diaries,* that put into words the type of social upheaval
that he and Nichols had come to see as inevitable.

Terry Nichols left the U.S. Army after a year. Despite a brief stay, he had made an impression on Timothy McVeigh. Nichols warned his platoon members that he would soon be recruiting for a different kind of army.

McVeigh saw an advertisement for the book in a gun magazine, promoting it as a source that would explain the status of the nation's gun laws. The ad for the book contained this headline: "What are you going to do when they take your guns?"

But instead, the book turned out to be a work of fiction. It was written by William L. Pierce, a white supremacist and organizer of the National Alliance, a West Virginia-based neo-Nazi group. Pierce published the book in 1978 under the pseudonym Andrew Macdonald; since then, it has rarely been sold in mainstream bookstores. Nevertheless, it has generated an underground cult following.

The Turner Diaries is a chilling account of a world gone mad. The book takes the form of a diary kept by a participant in the cataclysmic events that unfold. The story starts with the bombing of F.B.I. headquarters in Washington D.C.; soon, tensions escalate into a nuclear war between the United States and the former Soviet Union. The war results in the deaths of billions of people, wiping out virtually the entire populations of Europe, North America, South America, Africa, and Asia.

But there are survivors. Out of the nuclear holocaust an "Aryan Republic" forms. The society is based on the racist Nazi regime that came to power in Germany in the 1920s, eventually igniting World War II. At the end of World War II, Nazi dictator Adolf Hitler and his followers were defeated. In "The Turner Diaries," the Aryan survivors of the nuclear war triumph, forcing millions of Jews, African Americans, government officials, and other innocent people into slavery.

For Earl Turner, the main character, it's all worth it.

"For the first time I understood the deepest meaning of what we are doing," Turner says in the book. "I understand now why we cannot fail, no matter what we must do to win . . . . Everything that has been and everything that is yet to be depends on us. We are truly instruments of God in the fulfillment of His Grand Design. These may seem like strange words to be coming from me, who has never been religious, but they are utterly sincere words."

Timothy McVeigh read and reread *The Turner Diaries*. He bought several more copies and passed them out to his Army buddies. He thought it was the most important book he had ever read.

And then, on August 2, 1990, it seemed as though

Pierce's prophecy was about to come true. Iraqi dictator Saddam Hussein ordered an invasion into neighboring Kuwait. The United States and its allies quickly responded by organizing a huge multinational coalition of armies. For months, the coalition mobilized in the Persian Gulf, preparing to swoop down on the Iraqis. The First Infantry Division arrived in the Gulf in January 1991. For Timothy McVeigh, it meant he would finally have the chance to fire his weapon at something other than a target on an Army firing range or an empty soup can in his backyard.

Back in Fort Riley, McVeigh had trained as a gunner on a Bradley Fighting Vehicle. His zeal for soldiering and his skill as a marksman helped win him promotions in the short time he had served in the Army. McVeigh arrived at the Army base in Al Khobar, Saudi Arabia, a sergeant.

McVeigh's Bradley was assigned the job of preceding the much heavier and deadlier M-1 Abrams tanks onto the battlefield. Their role was to clear out resistance from Iraqi ground troops so that the M-1s could use their big guns on bunkers, missile launch pads, and other concentrations of Iraqi soldiers. It was a dangerous assignment, to be sure; the Bradleys would be heading into enemy fire first, taking the first hits in the attack. What's more, it was believed the Iraqis had laid down land mines, and that meant that if any explosives were hidden in the desert sand, the Bradleys would be first to find them.

"The Bradley has much less armor and is more susceptible to fire than the tank," McVeigh said later. "The tank commander reasoned that . . . if the Bradley goes first and blows up, the Abrams can come up behind and push it through, with its horsepower, and ignite any other mines that might not have been taken out . . . . In other words, he sent us in first as a sacrificial lamb. It happened to be my vehicle. You have the driver, gunner

and commander, and six troops in back. That's one of the decisions a military commander has to make, without regard for life. He decides those nine lives in the Bradley are worth doing it this way."

McVeigh spent several weeks in the Saudi desert waiting for the attack to begin. On January 17, 1991, after Saddam had resisted all calls to withdraw his troops from Kuwait, the coalition's leaders ordered the commencement of "Operation Desert Storm." For nearly six weeks, Air Force planes bombarded the Iraqi capital of Baghdad. Still, Saddam would not recall the invaders. Finally, on February 24, the ground war began. The coalition had mobilized nearly 700,000 troops in the Persian Gulf. Thousands of them flooded across the desert to engage the Iraqi invaders in combat.

A sergeant directs Bradley Fighting Vehicles in the Kuwaiti desert during training exercises. Timothy McVeigh became a gunner aboard a Bradley Fighting Vehicle and fought in Kuwait and Saudi Arabia during the Gulf War in the early 1990s.

McVeigh's Bradley was on the move in the predawn hours of February 24. The first sortie was not long in coming. McVeigh's Bradley encountered resistance after just 30 minutes of riding across the desert. The coalition soldiers had been told to expect hard-edged, zealous Iraqi fighting men. Instead, they found frightened, demoralized, poorly trained troops with no will to engage the enemy.

"On the first day, one of our tanks fired one round into the earth berm, thinking there was a tank behind it," McVeigh said. "As soon as he fired that shot, everybody in the Iraqi trenches surrendered. There was no tank back there. All these people were surrendering with their hands up."

Still, McVeigh would get his chance to fire at the enemy. On the second day of the ground assault, McVeigh's Bradley came upon an Iraqi position. The Bradley stopped more than a mile away, but using the vehicle's long-range optical equipment the commander could see a machine-gun nest hidden in the sand. McVeigh was given the order to fire.

The Bradley advanced and McVeigh trained his marksman's eye on the Iraqis. From a distance of nearly 4,000 feet, McVeigh fired off a round from the Bradley's 25-mm gun. Just as the round left the gun barrel, McVeigh saw an Iraqi soldier raise his head out of the sand.

McVeigh scored a direct hit on the Iraqi position.

"His head just disappeared," McVeigh said. "I saw everything above the shoulders disappear, like in a red mist. The guy next to him just dropped. In the military, you're supposed to stay at least five meters from anybody, at any time. That's the minimum fragmentation distance for some weapons."

Suddenly, the chatter over the military radios became alive with talk about McVeigh's shot. Dilly, who was riding in a nearby Bradley, said: "The amazing thing about that shot is, in a situation like that, the first round you fire is usually to help you zero in on the target. You watch where the first round lands, and then you adjust the second shot to hit the target. Tim hit this guy dead-on with the first shot. That's unheard of."

While McVeigh was finding adventure in the deserts of Kuwait and Saudi Arabia, Terry Nichols was finding a much different life. He returned home to Decker, Michigan, to resume an unhappy marriage. Again unable to carve out much of a career for himself, McVeigh divorced his wife and bounced from job to job, even working for a time as a ranch hand in Kansas. He also remarried, taking a young college student from the Philippines for his second wife.

While living in Michigan, though, Nichols had started attending meetings of the "Michigan Militia," a group of ultraconservative self-described "patriots" who harbored fears that the American government was intent on robbing them of their rights. Indeed, by the time Nichols started attending meetings in Michigan, the militia movement had spread throughout the country, attracting thousands of members who shared common, and decidedly unfounded, beliefs.

Some of the ideas raised by militia members were well known. Their arguments against gun control could be heard every day on virtually every conservative radio talk show on the air in America. Militia members believe gun control is contrary to the constitutional guarantees under the Second Amendment, and that the true purpose of gun control is to enable the government to disarm the citizens.

Other ideas are clearly far-fetched, that the government sends black helicopters over small towns to spy on

Norman Olsen (left) led the Michigan Militia in its campaign against gun control. The group feared the government's control over its citizens' lives had begun to spin wildly out of control. Around the time of the Oklahoma bombing, the Michigan Militia had gained widespread influence.

militia members, road signs include tiny bar codes intended to give foreign armies directions once they invade America, and that the ultimate goal of the federal government is to band together with other nations to form a single world government. They feel the government is too involved in citizens' everyday lives, imposing taxes and a myriad of laws and regulations that infringe on personal freedoms

"Within two years, I expect to see the Constitution suspended. We will be prepared to defend it," predicted Michigan Militia founder Norman Olson in 1995.

Olson's prediction, like so many of the militias' other theories, has yet to come true.

And yet, during the 1990s, militia membership mushroomed, reaching a pinnacle of as many as 100,000. Many of the members were drawn by the fiery rhetoric of their leaders who promised armed resistance against the government.

Among those groups were the Idaho-based United States Militia Association, whose leader, Samuel Sherwood, said: "Civil War could be coming, and with it the need to shoot Idaho legislators." Other groups included the Militia of Montana, the Indiana-based American Justice Federation, Constitutional Defense Militia of New Hampshire, and in North Carolina, Citizens for Reinstatement of Constitutional Government. Albert Esposito, the head of the North Carolina group, urged his followers to stockpile the four Bs: Bibles, bullets, beans, and bandages. The aim of the group, Esposito said, is to "Make the Holy Bible and the U.S. Constitution the law of the land." Still another group, the Florida State Militia, warned its members to "Buy ammo now! You won't be able to get it later!"

Soon, events would unfold just outside the town of Waco, Texas, that would convince militia members the federal government was, indeed, their enemy.

Waco

The Branch Davidian complex succumbs to flames on April 19, 1993. Federal agents attempted to smoke out the Davidians with tear gas, resulting in a fatal fire that ended the 51-day standoff. McVeigh took this incident as proof that the government planned to infringe on citizens' rights.

5

After leaving the Army, Timothy McVeigh returned to his father's home in Pendleton. His search for a good-paying job with a future proved futile. When McVeigh came home from the Persian Gulf he found a troubled American economy; factories in the depressed Buffalo area weren't hiring. And with no more than a high school diploma, McVeigh found few other doors open to him. He landed a job as a security guard, and stewed about the raw deal the government had delivered to the returning Persian Gulf veterans.

He stewed about a lot more as well. High taxes, crime in the streets, gun control, Jews, African Americans, imported goods, and politicians in general all seemed to raise his dander. On February 11, 1992, the *Lockport Union Sun and Journal* newspaper published a rather ominous letter to the editor written by McVeigh.

"America is in serious decline," McVeigh warned in his letter. "We have no proverbial tea to dump. Should we instead sink a ship full of Japanese imports? Is a civil war imminent? Do we have to shed blood to reform the current system? I hope it doesn't come to that, but it might."

At home, he was making his father nervous. On August 21, 1992, federal agents attempted a raid on a cabin in Ruby Ridge, Idaho, in an effort to arrest white separatist Randy Weaver on a charge of selling a sawed-off shotgun to an undercover agent.

Weaver refused to come out of the cabin. A gunfight ensued. During the exchange of gunfire, Weaver's 11-year-old son Sammy and wife Vicki were shot by federal agents. Also killed was William Degan, a United States marshal. Finally, after an 11-day standoff, Weaver surrendered.

For survivalists and militia members, the Ruby Ridge case became a rallying cry—proof that the federal government would stop at nothing to trample on people's rights. In Pendleton, McVeigh watched the events unfold on T.V. and was livid with rage. During the news coverage of the raid, McVeigh would get so angry that he'd shout profanities at the T.V. Bill McVeigh was troubled by the outbursts, but said little. "Timmy is strong willed," he would tell people.

By the end of 1992, Timothy McVeigh had decided to leave home. McVeigh itched to become part of what he perceived to be a growing revolution against the government of the United States. For months, McVeigh had been going to gun shows—not as a customer, but as a dealer. He also sold guns through the mail, dealing firearms through classified ads in gun magazines. Often, McVeigh would use the name "Tuttle" in the ads; he had seen the movie *Brazil*, a satire about citizens rising up against faceless, uncaring bureaucrats. The character of Tuttle, played by Robert DeNiro, was a gun-wielding urban terrorist who lived in the shadows.

Federal agents and reporters survey the contents of Randy Weaver's house. Authorities charged Weaver with illegally selling weapons; the 11-day siege ended in surrender. This episode, for McVeigh, marked another incident of government control.

Now, McVeigh planned to travel full time on the gun show circuit. He ordered dozens of copies of *The Turner Diaries* and offered them for sale on his table at a discount. For months, McVeigh lived in cheap motels or out of his car, selling guns and seeing the country. Whenever the gun show circuit took him to Arizona, he made time to visit his old Army pal Michael Fortier. In Michigan, he found Terry Nichols once again trying to make it as a farmer. The two men renewed their friendship. McVeigh even moved in with Nichols and his family for a time. They would stay up nights rehashing their old complaints about gun control and the government.

In the early months of 1993, McVeigh's attention turned to a news story that was starting to make it onto the front pages of newspapers. Just outside Waco, Texas, religious cult members under the leadership of a self-proclaimed messiah named David Koresh were refusing demands by federal agents to throw down their guns and surrender. To the militia movement, it seemed like the Ruby Ridge siege all over again. But they were wrong. This one would prove to be much worse.

■   ■   ■

David Koresh was born Vernon Wayne Howell in Houston, Texas, on August 17, 1959. He was the son of an unwed teenage mother. Vernon dropped out of high school himself, found work as an auto mechanic and played electric guitar in a rock and roll band.

He was also devoutly religious. In 1979 he joined the Seventh-Day Adventist Church in Tyler, Texas. He attended Bible studies and lived under the church's strict moral code; no use of tobacco or liquor and no premarital sex are allowed.

But Howell found himself at odds with church leaders—he would often interrupt services, striding to the pulpit to launch into tirades against the congregation's elders and demand that he be made a part of the church leadership. Finally, in 1984, the church elders told him he wasn't welcome back.

Howell searched for another church and soon found a congregation known as the "Branch Davidians"—a name borrowed from a group that had been formed in the 1930s by Victor Houteff, another Seventh-Day Adventist who split with the church. Howell became a popular member of the Branch Davidians; he was a natural leader and fiery speaker, and many members were drawn to his magnetic personality. In 1983, at the age of 24, he intended to marry 61-year-old Lois Roden, leader of the Branch Davidians. He never went through with the marriage and instead became a bigamist, marrying two young Branch-Davidian girls. Howell claimed multiple partners were permitted under biblical law. Both wives were under the age of 18.

By now, Howell found himself in a power struggle for control of the Davidians with George Roden, Lois's 45-year-old son. George Roden settled the matter by bringing the law down on Howell, accusing him of rape. Local authorities started looking into Howell's bigamist ways. In 1984, with investigators closing in, Howell left the Davidians and traveled out of state, but in 1988 he returned to Texas and convinced many members of the congregation to follow him to a patch of ground he purchased outside of Waco. When George Roden complained, Howell shot him. Later, Howell was acquitted on an attempted murder charge.

"He converted the leadership to Nazism," Roden later complained to reporters.

By the early 1990s, more than 100 Davidians were living in the complex of ramshackle cabins that Howell and his followers erected on the grounds. Howell had also changed his name to David Koresh, combining the names of two biblical kings; David, the second king of the Israelites, and Koresh, which is the Hebrew name for Cyrus, a Persian king who freed Jews from exile in Babylon, allowing them to return to their homeland in Israel. Now, the Davidians had taken on the look of a cult. They were totally devoted to Koresh, willing to give him their minds, their bodies, and ultimately, their lives.

"It's not just that he was enthralling," said Robert Scott, a Branch Davidian. "It's that everyone else was enthralled, and that made you feel that he must be special, that his message was Divine."

Still, folks near Waco got along with the Davidians. They paid their bills on time and often helped at nearby farms. Unknown to local residents, though, Koresh and his followers were stockpiling guns. The Davidians would attend gun shows throughout the Southwest. At one show in Houston, Koresh laid down $7,000 in cash to buy a .50-mm caliber semiautomatic machine gun and 100 rounds of ammunition. He called his grandmother after the show and said, "Grandma, it's coming a time, I'm going to bring you a little gun."

Koresh and the Davidians would practice target shooting at their compound, which raised the interest of the local police. Soon, the police called in the Bureau of Alcohol, Tobacco, and Firearms (A.T.F.). To investigate, the A.T.F. sent a spy into the compound. Agent Robert Rodriguez pretended to be a devoted Branch Davidian; he lived among the cult members for several months, and observed that they had gathered together quite an arsenal of illegal weapons and explosives.

On February 28, 1993, A.T.F. agents planned a raid on the Branch-Davidian compound. But things went wrong from the start. Hours before the raid, dozens of agents from the A.T.F. as well as other law enforcement agencies began mobilizing in town. Waco is not a big city; the large police force did not go unnoticed by local residents, and there was no question where they were headed: the Branch Davidian compound.

Koresh was ready for them. As a team of A.T.F. agents approached a building they were met by a barrage of gunfire. "(We) came under heavy and sustained firepower for over half an hour," said A.T.F. agent John Killorin. "We were literally trying to move into position when they opened fire."

Four federal agents and six Davidians died in the gunfire. When the shooting stopped, Koresh and the

David Koresh, leader of the Branch Davidians, had McVeigh's support in his quest to stockpile explosives and guns.

A.T.F. agents spoke by telephone and agreed to hold their fire. For the next 51 days, federal agents and Branch Davidians endured a standoff.

Outside the compound, the confrontation was drawing quite a crowd. Dozens of news reporters and T.V. camera crews as well as hundreds of spectators flocked to Waco. Certainly, many people headed to Waco so they could watch a news event unfold. But many others, with ties to the militia movement, also gathered outside the police barriers to give their vocal and moral support to the Davidians, whom they regarded as heroes standing up for the right to own guns. One of the Davidians' most zealous supporters was Timothy McVeigh.

McVeigh followed the story on T.V. and in the newspapers, then decided that he couldn't sit still. He loaded his car with antigovernment brochures and bumper stickers, then headed for Waco where he planned to tell anyone who would listen that the government had gone too far this time.

Police wouldn't let him anywhere near the Davidian compound, so he hung around Waco for a few days, displaying his brochures and bumper stickers on the hood of his car. They carried such messages as "Fear the Government that Fears Your Gun" and "When Guns are Outlawed, I Will Become an Outlaw." Few people noticed him or seemed very interested in what he had to say; certainly, Timothy McVeigh was far from the most interesting thing happening in Waco.

But he did draw the attention of a student news reporter. Michelle Rauch worked for the school newspaper at nearby Southern Methodist University, and she drove to Waco during her spring break in search of an offbeat story. She found her story in Timothy McVeigh.

"He said he just came in response to the standoff and that he went on to say that he was opposed to how they handled the initial raid, that he thought it would be more appropriate had just the local sheriff gone down and issued an arrest warrant," Rauch recalled. "He was just sitting on the hood of his car. He was willing to talk to me . . . . I found it very useful. He had a lot of views that he shared with me, which is—as a writer and a journalist—I enjoyed speaking with him to write about his views in my article."

And McVeigh had little trouble articulating his views to the young reporter. He told her "The A.T.F. just wants a chance to play with their toys, paid for by government money" and that "The government is afraid of the guns people have because they have to have control of the people at all times. Once you take away the guns, you can do anything to the people."

McVeigh told Rauch the Davidian standoff is only the beginning and people should watch the government's role and heed the warning signs.

"I believe we are slowly turning into a socialist government," McVeigh said. "The government is continually growing bigger and more powerful, and the people need to prepare to defend themselves against government control."

Rauch published her interview with McVeigh in her school newspaper on March 30. McVeigh didn't hang around Texas long enough to read his name in the newspaper. Growing bored with the standoff, and frustrated by his inability to interest anyone other than a college newspaper reporter in his opinions, McVeigh headed first to Arizona to spend time with his old Army buddy, Michael Fortier, who lived in a mobile home in the desert. After a few weeks, McVeigh headed east, stopping first in Tulsa, Oklahoma, to attend a gun show, and then in Decker, Michigan, to see Terry Nichols. He arrived at the Nichols farm in mid-April, just as things were ready to explode in Waco.

On April 18, 1993, McVeigh decided to return to Waco, and convinced Nichols to accompany him. Nichols' brother, James, also lived at the farm, and was angry as well at the government's antics. The next morning, April 19, McVeigh crawled under his car to change the oil. He planned to leave for Waco the next day and wanted to make sure the car was ready for the long drive. Suddenly, McVeigh heard shouting from the farmhouse.

"Tim! Tim!" someone shouted. "Get in here! It's on fire!"

McVeigh rushed into the house and found the Nichols brothers staring at the scene on their T.V. The Davidian complex was in flames.

The story of what happened soon emerged. During the standoff, 35 Davidians decided to leave the complex and turn themselves in. As they came out, they were taken into custody and questioned by federal agents. They told the agents that sanitary conditions were deteriorating inside the compound, food was running out, and Koresh had been beating the children. So the F.B.I. and A.T.F. agents developed a plan to storm the complex. The agents would shoot "C.S.," a potent tear gas, into the complex buildings, forcing Koresh and the others to leave the buildings where a force of some 170 federal officers would be waiting for them. Meanwhile, a team of Bradley Fighting Vehicles would drive onto the grounds and smash down the walls of the complex. U.S. Attorney General Janet Reno approved the plan, and the siege was set for the predawn hours of April 19.

Just before 6 A.M., an F.B.I. agent read a statement over a loudspeaker directed at the complex. The statement said: "There's going to be tear gas injected into the compound. This is not an assault. Do not fire. The idea is to get you out of the compound."

The tear gas was shot into the compound. The Bradleys advanced and were met by gunfire from the compound. Tear gas was again lobbed into the compound. Still, no one emerged from the buildings. For six hours, the F.B.I. lobbed C.S. gas into the compound, and yet was unable to force any of the Davidians out of their hiding places.

And then, shortly after noon, smoke started seeping out of the buildings. Within seconds, the compound was engulfed in flames. Some of the Davidians made it to safety, but most died in the fire. Koresh's charred body was found in the rubble; he died from a gunshot wound to the head. The medical examiner was never able to tell if Koresh committed suicide or if someone else shot the leader of the Branch Davidians. The final death total was 86 people, including 17 children.

For McVeigh, the government had finally gone too far. No longer content with handing out pamphlets and

bumper stickers or selling *The Turner Diaries* at gun shows, McVeigh decided that the time had come for direct action.

In Decker, McVeigh started attending meetings of the Michigan Militia along with Terry and James Nichols. The militia was urging its members to store weapons and food to prepare for the final breakdown of the social order, but McVeigh and the Nichols brothers started advocating that the militia take the next step—revolution.

That was too radical an idea even for the Michigan Militia. Normal Olson listened to their ideas, then told McVeigh and the Nichols brothers not to come to any more meetings.

Later, Olson said, "These people were told to leave because of that type of talk of destruction and harm and terrorism."

The Michigan Militia, led by Norman Olsen, advocated Second Amendment rights and preparing for social breakdown. But, when Timothy McVeigh and Terry Nichols proposed a revolution, Olsen told them the Michigan Militia did not support them.

"Something Big is Going to Happen"

6

For two days, McVeigh sat in the Noble County jail north of Oklahoma City. Trooper Charles Hanger had taken McVeigh there after arresting him along Interstate 35 for carrying a concealed weapon without a license and driving without a license plate. They were minor charges, and McVeigh was promised that he would soon have the opportunity to appear before a judge for a bail hearing. McVeigh knew that bail would be set low, and he would be freed from jail.

Meanwhile, as rescue workers struggled to find survivors of the Murrah bombing, law enforcement agents were busy as well. Many of them were sifting through the rubble in Oklahoma City searching for clues. Others were tracking down hundreds of leads that had been phoned in by well-meaning people who believed they had seen something or somebody suspicious in the final few minutes before the blast.

The F.B.I.'s initial suspicion fell on foreign terrorists. The explosion at the Murrah building happened just two years after a group of Arab terrorists set off a bomb in the parking garage below the World Trade Center in New York City. Soon, though, the clues started pointing toward other suspects.

One block from the Murrah building, police found the rear axle of a truck that had crashed into a car. Obviously, the truck had been very close to the scene of the blast. Still intact on the truck remnant was the Vehicle Identification Number (V.I.N.) for the truck—a series of numerals inscribed on the axle by the manufacturer. And then, police found the front bumper from a cargo truck with the license plate still intact. Computer checks soon confirmed that the license plate and V.I.N. were from the same truck—a Ryder Rental Inc. vehicle that had been leased in Junction City, Kansas, by a man named Robert Kling.

Federal agents hurried to the Junction City car rental agency and talked with employees there, who described Kling and another man who accompanied him into the rental office on April 17 to lease the truck. Based on the descriptions, police artists were able to draw sketches of Kling and the other man. With the sketches in hand, police combed Junction City in search of the two men.

On April 20, the day after the explosion, police interviewed Lea McGown, the manager of the Dreamland Motel in Junction City. She identified the picture of Kling as somebody who had stayed in Room 25 recently, but he didn't register under that name. McGown told police he used the name "Timothy McVeigh." She also told police that McVeigh had parked a large, yellow Ryder truck in the Dreamland Motel parking lot. McGown found McVeigh's registration form in the Dreamland's files.

When he checked into the motel, McVeigh listed his home address as the farm of Terry Nichols in Decker, Michigan.

While investigators headed for Decker, other agents searched for McVeigh. Police departments throughout the country were sent his description and asked to be on the watch for him. At F.B.I. headquarters in Washington D.C., agents fed his name into the National Crime Information Computer, a national database that tells police the status of all fugitives and others that police wish to question. They quickly learned that a man named Timothy McVeigh had been arrested on April 19 just north of Oklahoma City by a highway patrolman. A call was made to the Noble County jail. Was McVeigh still in custody? Sheriff Jerry R. Cook checked his records.

"Yeah," he said. "We got him incarcerated."

The agents told Cook that McVeigh was a prime suspect in the Murrah bombing and that he was not to

Authorities used this truck axle to trace the exploded Ryder truck back to Timothy McVeigh. Investigators found the axle pictured here on the ground near a damaged car nearly one block from where the truck exploded.

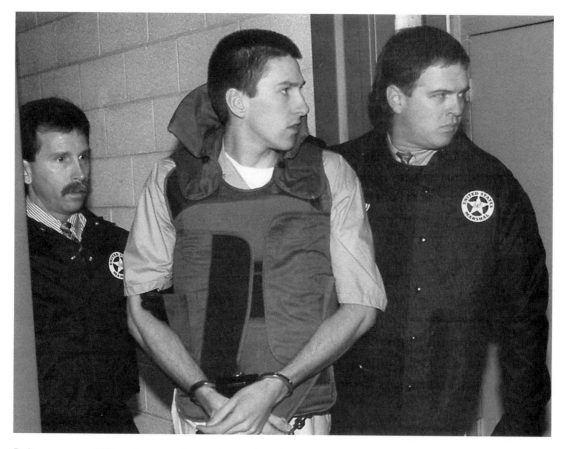

Police arrested Timothy McVeigh on unrelated charges just after the explosion. Authorities kept him in custody while they learned about McVeigh's hatred for the government from Terry Nichols, his brother James Nichols, and many others.

be released. They hurried to Noble County.

Cook decided to check on McVeigh. He went to McVeigh's cell in the county jail and found him missing. Cook rushed to the Noble County Courthouse, where he learned that McVeigh was in the holding cell and scheduled to appear before a judge within minutes for a bail hearing. Cook suspected that the charges against McVeigh were minor and the judge would release McVeigh on minimal bail. He found an assistant district attorney and told him of the F.B.I.'s interest in McVeigh. The hearing was quickly postponed. McVeigh was returned to his cell.

Police were also closing in on the Nichols brothers. In Decker, they found James Nichols living on the farm, and learned that Terry Nichols had moved some months before to Herington, Kansas. Before they could catch up with him, though, Terry Nichols walked into the Herington Police Station and turned himself in.

F.B.I. agents were called in, and they met with Nichols. For nine hours, Terry Nichols told them all he knew about Timothy McVeigh. After Waco, Nichols said, McVeigh swore that he would make the government pay for what he regarded as the murders of the Branch Davidians. For two years, he said, McVeigh had been unsure of what steps to take, but as April 19 approached—the two-year anniversary of the Waco siege—it was clear that McVeigh was planning to act.

On April 16, Nichols said, McVeigh called him at his Herington home and told Nichols he was in Oklahoma City. McVeigh said he needed to get to Junction City, some 270 miles away, to pick up a rented Ryder truck he had left in the parking lot of the Dreamland Motel. McVeigh asked Nichols to take him to Junction City.

"Something big is going to happen," McVeigh told Nichols.

Nichols gave McVeigh the ride. On April 18, McVeigh called again. This time, the two men drove the Ryder truck to a storage shed in Herington that Nichols had leased. Inside the shed, Nichols stored bags of ammonium nitrate, a chemical commonly used as a fertilizer. Also inside were an antitank rocket, 33 guns, bomb detonators, 55-gallon plastic drums, books about the Waco incident and antigovernment pamphlets. Nichols told the F.B.I. that he helped McVeigh load the fertilizer and the detonators in the truck, then went home. A day later, Nichols said, he heard about the Murrah blast.

But there was a lot that Nichols left out of the story, and it didn't take long for investigators to fill in the missing parts. They determined that Nichols learned how to make fertilizer bombs while growing up on a farm. By mixing ammonium nitrate with fuel oil, Nichols knew, a particularly volatile bomb could be concocted. Farmers have used small fertilizer bombs for years to clear tree stumps off their grounds.

McVeigh and Nichols had been buying ammonium nitrate for months prior to the Murrah blast. The F.B.I. also linked McVeigh, Nichols, and Michael Fortier to the November 1994 robbery of an Arkansas gun dealer named Roger Moore, whom McVeigh had befriended on the gun show circuit. Nichols and McVeigh broke into Moore's house and stole more than $60,000, the F.B.I. charged, to raise money for their plan. A month later, the three men visited Oklahoma City, where McVeigh identified the Murrah building as the target. Finally, the F.B.I. concluded that on April 18, 1995, one day before the blast, McVeigh and Nichols constructed a 7,000-pound ammonium nitrate bomb in the cargo hold of the Ryder truck at Geary Lake State Park in Kansas. Finally, the F.B.I. determined, McVeigh parked the Ryder truck in front of the Murrah building just before 9 A.M. on April 19, set off a timer on the bomb's detonator and walked away. He had parked the Mercury Marquis on an Oklahoma City street, and used it as a getaway car following the explosion. In fact, numerous emergency vehicles passed him as he drove away from the scene and headed north on Interstate 35. When police searched the Mercury following McVeigh's arrest, they found a copy of *The Turner Diaries* as well as several antigovernment pamphlets.

On August 10, federal prosecutors announced they had charged Timothy McVeigh and Terry Nichols with constructing a weapon of mass destruction and using it to destroy a federal building and killing 168 people. The men were charged with the murders of the eight federal agents killed in the building. The murders of the 160 others in the building were not federal crimes—those were state offenses that were out of the jurisdiction of federal law. If convicted of the charges, McVeigh and Nichols would face the death penalty.

Michael Fortier was implicated as well. He was charged with being aware of the plot and concealing it from authorities, lying to the F.B.I., and participating in the robbery that financed the plan. Finally, James Nichols was indicted as well. He was charged with conspiring with his brother and McVeigh to make an unregistered destructive device.

The charges against James Nichols were eventually dropped for lack of evidence. Michael Fortier pleaded guilty and agreed to testify against McVeigh and Terry Nichols in court. For agreeing to cooperate, Fortier received a sentence of 12 years in prison, about half the maximum he could have received.

Terry Nichols maintained that he helped construct the bomb but had nothing to do with picking a target, and had no knowledge McVeigh intended to use the bomb to kill people. The jury convicted him of conspiracy and involuntary manslaughter, finding that he did not intend to kill. Judge Richard P. Matsch, who would also preside over McVeigh's trial, sentenced Nichols to life in prison.

But McVeigh refused to make a bargain with the government he hated so much. His case headed for trial.

On March 19, 1997, the case of *United States v. Timothy McVeigh* convened in Denver, Colorado. McVeigh's lawyer, Stephen Jones, had asked for what's known as a "change of venue" because he didn't believe his client could receive a fair trial in Oklahoma City. Under law, criminal defendants are entitled to be tried in the place where the crime was committed, but in some circumstances the court will agree to move the trial. Jones pointed out that nearly everyone in Oklahoma City harbored a resentment toward McVeigh and, therefore, it would be impossible to find fair and impartial jurors. The court agreed, and the trial was moved to Denver.

Just before the trial started, a newspaper in Dallas, Texas, published a story reporting that McVeigh admitted his guilt to Jones and other defense lawyers. *The Dallas Morning News* claimed it had obtained memos written by Jones and attorneys assisting him in which McVeigh made a full confession. The story said that a defense lawyer asked McVeigh why he hadn't set the bomb off at night to minimize casualties. According to the newspaper, McVeigh responded: "That would not have gotten the point across to the government. We needed a body count to make our point."

Despite the publicity generated by the so-called "confession," Jones and federal prosecutor Joseph Hartzler were able to select seven men and five women to serve on the jury.

Testimony before Judge Matsch commenced on April 24. In Denver, the courtroom was packed—mostly with news reporters from across the country assigned to cover the trial. In Oklahoma City, victims of the explosion and their families were permitted to watch the trial in an auditorium via closed-circuit T.V.

During the trial, McVeigh was housed in a specially designed prison cell in the federal courthouse. To ensure his security, the cell had no windows. However, federal marshals were able to observe him through video cameras installed in the walls. Every morning, he was escorted by no less than 50 federal marshals to the courtroom.

In his opening statement to the jury, Hartzler made it clear what the case would be about: Timothy McVeigh, aided by Terry Nichols, planted a bomb in front of the Murrah building that killed 168 people, including 19 children in the day-care center. McVeigh committed the

Terry Nichols received a life sentence for his involvement in the bombing. Michael Fortier, a third man implicated by authorities, testified against Nichols and McVeigh in exchange for a light sentence— 12 years in jail.

crime, Hartzler said, to get back at the government for the siege on the Branch Davidian complex in Waco. Hartzler argued that McVeigh was inspired to plant the bomb by what he had read in *The Turner Diaries.*

"You will hear evidence in this case that McVeigh liked to consider himself a patriot, someone who could start the second American Revolution," Hartzler said. "The literature in his car quoted statements from the Founding Fathers and other people who played a part in the American Revolution, people like Patrick Henry and Samuel Adams. McVeigh isolated and took these statements out of context, and he did that to justify his antigovernment violence."

"Well, ladies and gentlemen, the statements of our forefathers can never . . . justify warfare against innocent children. Our forefathers didn't fight British women and children. They fought other soldiers. They fought them face to face, hand to hand."

Witness after witness took the stand. Many of the witnesses were survivors of the blast, who described how they fought their way out of the rubble. Ambulance workers and firemen described the scene they found when they responded to the emergency call. Local police and F.B.I. agents talked about the investigation and the clues that led them to McVeigh.

Michael Fortiers' wife Lori testified how McVeigh talked about blowing up a federal building when he visited the Fortier's mobile home in Arizona. She told the jurors that McVeigh sat on the floor of the mobile home and stacked soup cans, explaining how he planned to arrange the explosives he would use. On April 19, 1995, when she saw reports of the Murrah explosion on T.V., Lori said, "I knew right away it was Tim."

Michael Fortier testified that McVeigh told him he had selected the Murrah building for the blast because he believed the orders to raid the Davidian compound had originated in the Bureau of Alcohol, Tobacco, and Firearms office on the ninth floor, a notion that was incorrect. Perhaps Fortier's most chilling testimony concerned McVeigh's justification for the bombing. He said, "He considered all those people to be as if they were the storm troopers in the movie *Star Wars*. They may be individually innocent, but because they are part of the Evil Empire, they were guilty by association."

It took a month for Hartzler to present the government's case. Jones took just four days to present the defense. Jones offered little evidence in rebuttal to the prosecution's case; instead, he told the jurors that foreign terrorists were responsible for the bombing, and that his client was the government's scapegoat because the F.B.I. had failed to track down the true killers.

Jones attacked the testimony of Michael and Lori Fortier, claiming they fabricated their stories to win sweet deals from prosecutors. He pointed out that Michael received a reduced sentence and Lori walked away with no charges at all.

"Someone blew up the Murrah building," Jones told jurors. "But more likely than not, several people were involved. They had skill and training, and they didn't get it out of some book that talks about mixing it in an oven."

Timothy McVeigh did not take the stand to testify in his own defense.

The jurors retired to deliberate on May 30. Four days later, they reached a verdict: McVeigh was guilty of all charges.

Next came the penalty phase of the trial, in which the jurors decide the sentence. Jones asked for life imprisonment, arguing that his client had led a law-abiding life prior to the bombing, that he had served in the Gulf War, and that he had been motivated to commit the crime through political beliefs rather than a personal vendetta aimed at a particular victim or a desire to obtain money.

The jurors were unmoved. After two days of deliberations, the jury settled on a punishment: Death.

"Our Grief Has Turned to Anger"

Gary Gilmore was a career criminal who had led a violent life. Most of his adult years were spent in and out of prison. In 1976, he was convicted of murdering two men in Utah and sentenced to death.

A year later, Gilmore told his lawyers he was no longer interested in pursuing his appeals, which were sure to be lengthy. Gilmore said he could not bear the prospect of spending the next several years behind bars, and he asked the state of Utah to carry out the jury's verdict.

The state obliged. On January 17, 1977, Gilmore was blindfolded, strapped to a chair in an unused cannery serving as the death chamber, and executed by firing squad—the state's legislated method of dispatching death row inmates.

"Death is the only inescapable, unavoidable sure thing," Gilmore said shortly before the execution. "We are sentenced to die the day we're born."

Gilmore was the first American executed in 10 years. In the late 1960s, death penalty opponents had managed to stall executions while they challenged the laws permitting them. Finally, in a landmark 1972 case, the United States Supreme Court struck down every death penalty statute in America, ruling them unconstitutional. The Supreme Court found that the nation's death penalty laws were in violation of the Eighth Amendment's guarantee against "cruel and unusual punishment." Specifically, the court ruled that juries had too much discretion in deciding who should receive the death penalty and for what reason. In response, the states rewrote their death penalty laws, requiring guidelines for juries in death penalty cases. Now, juries would be guided by "aggravating" and "mitigating" factors during the sentencing phases of death penalty trials.

In McVeigh's case, the prosecution argued that the aggravating factors included the sheer enormity of the crime as well as McVeigh's desire to rebel against the government. The defense countered that the mitigating factors the jury should consider included McVeigh's military service and his prior record as a law-abiding citizen. Clearly, the jury decided that the aggravating factors outweighed the mitigating circumstances, and sentenced him to death.

When the Supreme Court ruled the death penalty statutes unconstitutional in 1972, its order commuted to life imprisonment the sentences of more than 600 inmates awaiting their executions. No defendant sentenced prior to the Supreme Court ruling could now be executed. The moratorium that lasted until Gilmore's execution in 1977 marked the end of the first extended period in the nation's history that the death penalty had not been imposed.

Indeed, the first man executed on American soil was George Kendall, a Jamestown colonist who was hanged in 1608 after he was convicted of spying for Spain. In those days, such minor offenses as stealing crops, killing chickens, and trading with Indians could result in a noose around the neck of the perpetrator. During the next four centuries, Americans would define certain crimes they felt deserved the death penalty, murder being chief among them. Over the years, though, other crimes, such as treason and rape, were regarded as death penalty crimes.

In the late 1800s and early 1900s Americans started rethinking the death penalty. Many people believed it was a barbaric form of punishment for a civilized society. By 1917, six states had actually outlawed the death penalty. Meanwhile, in the states where the death penalty still existed, some thought was given to the method of execution. For years, capital punishment had been carried out through hangings. In 1890, New York State first used the electric chair, which was regarded as a quicker and less painful way for the condemned prisoner to meet his fate. Many other states soon installed electric chairs in their own death rows. Others turned to the use of cyanide gas released as the condemned criminal sat strapped in a closed, air-tight chamber. Eventually, death by lethal injection became the standard method of dispatching the condemned.

In the 1920s, in response to the anarchist movement in the United States as well as the violent crime wave caused by Prohibition, judges and juries started to become much less forgiving. States that abolished the death penalty reinstated their statutes, and by the 1930s nearly 170 inmates a year were being executed.

When the Supreme Court ruled the states' death

penalty statutes unconstitutional in 1972, it threw out the federal government's death penalty law as well. Congress responded by writing a new federal death statute, establishing execution as the punishment for such crimes as murder of a government official, a kidnapping that results in death, treason, and running a large-scale drug operation. Later, President Bill Clinton signed the 1994 Violent Crime Control and Law Enforcement Act that expanded the death penalty to some 60 crimes, most of which involved murder. And in 1996, in response to the Murrah building bombing, President Clinton signed the Anti-Terrorism and Effective Death Penalty Act of 1996, which limits the legal rights of terrorists convicted of murdering Americans, effectively speeding up their trials and, of course, their punishments.

In extraordinary circumstances, the American military has been called in. After Arab extremists killed more than 3,000 people in the September 2001 attacks on the World Trade Center and Pentagon, President George W. Bush announced a wide-sweeping war on terrorism. The first target was terrorist leader Osama bin Laden and the Taliban government of Afghanistan that protected him. The American military was dispatched to Afghanistan to bring down the Taliban and root out bin Laden.

"Our grief has turned to anger, and anger to resolution," Bush said shortly after the terrorist attack. "Whether we bring our enemies to justice, or bring justice to our enemies, justice will be done."

Sometimes, the government has failed to act. Timothy McVeigh started buying guns on the gun show circuit and later became a gun dealer himself. Such shows can be found in many American cities every weekend. Promoters lease a hotel ballroom or similar venue, then permit gun dealers to set up tables and sell their wares to gun enthusiasts. Such shows are largely unregulated and do

The second tower of the World Trade Center erupts in flames as a hijacked plane plows into the side of it on September 11, 2001. Both towers of the World Trade Center eventually crumbled in the terrorist attacks, prompting the president of the United States, George W. Bush, to declare war on terrorism.

not fall under the restrictions of the Brady Law that require cooling-off periods and background checks before the gun can be obtained by the customer.

In 1999, two students at Columbine High School in Littleton, Colorado, convinced an adult friend to buy guns for them at a gun show. Dylan Klebold and Eric Harris later took their weapons to school, where they commenced a shooting rampage that left 12 students and one teacher dead before they turned the guns on themselves. Following the Columbine massacre, many lawmakers and gun control activists called for legislation that would place Brady Law-style restrictions on gun shows, but lobbyists for the National Rifle Association and other progun groups succeeded in stalling the legislation.

"I think gun shows and swap meets are a serious problem," said Susan Pollack, a director of Handgun Control Inc., a gun control lobbying group. "We know that many felons and juveniles shop them without background checks."

Nevertheless, terrorism in America has resulted in some restrictions on citizens. Following the World Trade Center and Pentagon attacks, security was stepped up at American airports because the terrorists had hijacked commercial airliners for use in their suicide missions. Even before those incidents, however, the federal government had already taken steps to protect its buildings and employees from attack. In the U.S. Capitol in Washington D.C., visitors must pass through metal detectors before they can enter the House and Senate galleries while some corridors of the Capitol are completely off-limits to anyone who doesn't work there. In the parking lots outside the nearby House and Senate office buildings, huge concrete barriers have been installed, which are intended to prevent a suicide bomber from ramming his vehicle into the buildings. Across town, at the White House,

Pennsylvania Avenue is closed to traffic to prevent a suicide bomber from driving a vehicle laden with explosives through the front gates of the Executive Mansion. At other government installations throughout the country, police have closed streets surrounding buildings.

As lawmakers find themselves coming to terms with the Murrah building explosion as well as the World Trade Center and Pentagon attacks, they also realize that America is a free and open society. The U.S. Constitution guarantees the right of free speech as well as the freedom of movement. Law enforcement officers know they must respect people's rights. The Constitution guarantees no illegal searches or seizures, which means police must have "probable cause" to believe a crime is being planned or committed before they break down the door of a suspected terrorist.

Indeed, lawmakers will have to find ways to preserve people's rights while still guaranteeing protection for Americans against terrorism.

■　　　■　　　■

Following McVeigh's conviction, he was transported to Florence, Colorado, to await execution in the federal government's most secure prison, the U.S. Penitentiary Administrative Maximum, known as "Supermax." The $60 million, 480-cell prison opened in 1995 to house the nation's most dangerous federal inmates. He would wait at Supermax for his appeals to run their course.

In Oklahoma City, McVeigh left behind hundreds of survivors and family members of the victims. As he awaited his approaching execution date, they waited as well for the moment when the executioner would carry out the verdict of the court, bringing finality to their saga.

Amy Petty was buried under tons of rubble at the

Murrah building but was miraculously rescued. Following the bombing, Petty found herself plagued by survivor's guilt. She asked herself why she was spared while so many friends had died.

"I think the very most difficult part was returning to work," she said. "I'm now vice president of operations. It's kind of bittersweet. Because every time I get a promotion I think, 'So-and-so would have been in line for this next.' That's kind of hard to take sometimes."

Susan Walton survived as well, but faced years of medical procedures. Following the blast, Walton was forced to undergo 26 surgeries as well as long painful periods of rehabilitation. Over the years, she managed to go from a wheelchair to crutches to a cane. During that time, she found herself overwhelmed by people's generosity.

"I didn't have any insurance at the time, so basically most of my care has been given through donations," she said. "The doctors—a lot of them—have donated their services. They fixed our house up for us. A lot of times you send your money and you don't know where it's going, but they built on a handicapped bathroom for me. Basically, anything I've needed has been provided for me."

Don Hull was an Oklahoma City policeman. On the morning of April 19, 1995, he rushed to the scene of the explosion and started pulling victims out of the rubble. Thoughts of that morning continued to haunt him.

He said, "My worst nightmare to this day: my daughter was three at the time, and I remember going through the rubble and I found a hand. Just a hand. It fit in the palm of my hand. And I dug and dug, because I had to find the rest that went with this hand. I never did. But that bothered me more than anything. Because that hand was the exact same size as my daughter's."

Survivor Ann Banks admitted to having a great deal

of trouble facing down her fears following the Murrah blast. Banks worked in the Housing and Urban Development office on the eighth floor when the bomb destroyed the building.

"My son lives in Atlanta, and he sent me a package on Mother's Day," Banks recalled in 1997. "It was delivered by Federal Express. The man rang the doorbell and told me he had this package for me. I told him I couldn't take it. My thinking was, it may be a bomb. I told the man, 'Just set it down in the middle of the front yard, and I will sign for it. But I can't take the package.' My son called to see if I had received his gift. I told him, 'Yes, I sure did, and it's sitting in the middle of the front yard.' And he coached me: 'Mother, it's from me. Just look at the package. What does it say? Does it say it's from your son?' I said, 'Yes, it does.' 'Is your name on the front of it?' I said, 'Yes, it is.' He said, 'Well, just pick it up.' I did. I said, 'I'll go in and get some scissors and I'll come back out and I'll take the paper wrapping off of it.' That's what I did. I opened it outside and saw that he had sent me a beautiful little jogging set for Mother's Day."

Captain of
His Soul

Super maximum prisons, which share the nickname Supermax, house the nation's most dangerous criminals. Timothy McVeigh awaited his sentence in Colorado's Supermax alongside both Terry Nichols and Fortier.

At Supermax, Timothy McVeigh found himself in rather famous company. Other inmates housed at the prison included Theodore Kaczynski and Ramzi Ahmed Yousef. Kaczynski was the notorious "Unabomber" who had killed three people and injured 10 in a series of attacks through letter bombs he mailed to individuals. Yousef was one of the masterminds of the 1993 World Trade Center bombing.

Michael Fortier and Terry Nichols were also at Supermax. Although Fortier testified against him, and Nichols confessed, providing police with evidence in the case, McVeigh harbored no resentment against the two men. In fact, he sought them out, anxious to clear up the one question that had been troubling him since the bomb was detonated on April 19, 1995: Did they know there was a day-care center in the building?

Fortier had been in the building before the explosion. He claimed to have had no knowledge that there were children in the building. Nichols avoided McVeigh; the two men would never compare notes.

Still, McVeigh maintained that he never knew of the existence of the day-care center. He said that it was unfortunate that children had to die in the blast, but he had no remorse about setting off the bomb, and that the act was necessary to show the government that citizens would not tolerate the loss of their rights.

He said: "My decision to take human life at the Murrah building—I did not do it for personal gain. I ease my mind in that . . . . I did it for the larger good."

The 19 dead children, McVeigh said, were "collateral damage."

■   ■   ■

In Oklahoma City, the federal government constructed a memorial to the victims of the Murrah bombing. On the site of the former federal building, 168 bronze chairs were erected to honor them. Also standing on the site is the "Survivor Tree," a broad elm that stood on the Murrah grounds prior to the explosion and managed to survive the building's collapse. Elsewhere in Oklahoma City, the federal government made plans to erect a new federal building. After the blast, the services offered by the Housing and Urban Development department, the Department of Agriculture, and other agencies were still needed by the people of Oklahoma. With no building to house them, the federal government was forced to find temporary facilities for those agencies throughout the region. This time, the new federal building was designed to resist terrorism—the facility would include security cameras, concrete barriers to keep cars away from the entrance and laminated glass that would not fly out of the

BAYLEE ALMON

Charles Porter IV worked as a credit officer at an Oklahoma City bank, deciding whether to make loans to people. As a hobby, he took photographs. On the morning of April 19, 1995, he was driving in downtown Oklahoma City when he heard the explosion at the Alfred P. Murrah Federal Building.

Porter rushed to the scene, grabbed his camera from his car trunk, and started taking pictures. One of the pictures he took was of Oklahoma City fireman Chris Fields carrying the limp body of one-year-old Baylee Almon out of the Murrah building debris.

Later that day, Porter took his film to a local Wal-Mart for developing. Next he headed to the Oklahoma City bureau of the Associated Press (A.P.), the international organization that provides news stories and photographs to thousands of newspapers.

He showed his photos to editors at the A.P. bureau. They bought several pictures, including the photograph of Fields carrying the baby.

The next day, Porter's photograph of Chris Fields and Baylee Almon appeared on the front pages of newspapers throughout the world, capturing in one dramatic image the overwhelming horror and sadness of that morning in Oklahoma City. Later, Vin Alabisio, A.P. vice president and executive photo editor, said Porter's picture "forced a world to reflect on the devastating toll exacted by an act of terrorism."

Nearly a year later, Porter's photograph won the Pulitzer Prize, America's most prestigious award for journalism. The prize was established a century ago by Joseph Pulitzer, a wealthy and influential newspaper publisher. Rarely is the award presented to somebody who doesn't make his living in journalism.

"Obviously, I'm very very excited and very honored because I'm realizing how prestigious this award is," said Porter, shortly after he won the Pulitzer. "I'm torn because of the picture. I don't want to lose sight of the fact that this picture represents anyone and everyone who was involved in this tragedy."

Porter said he couldn't bring himself to celebrate winning the Pulitzer Prize.

Sadly, Baylee Almon did not survive the Murrah building blast. She was one of 19 children in the Murrah building day-care center who died when the bomb exploded.

Baylee's mother Aren Almon was a single parent struggling to support herself and her child. On the morning of the tragedy, Aren had just dropped her daughter off at the day-care center before heading to her job at an insurance company. When she heard the rumble of the bomb explode in the distance, Aren's first thought was that a thunderstorm was sweeping through the area.

"We heard that they found a baby with yellow booties, and I knew it was her," Aren said.

Soon after the photo appeared in the press, Aren started receiving letters of condolence. In fact, she received more than 2,000 letters from as far away as England, Australia, and Guam.

In the days following the tragedy, Aren Almon fought hard to keep her privacy. She turned down many requests by reporters and T.V. talk shows for interviews, and barred the press from her daughter's funeral. She also found it necessary to hire a lawyer to fight against the unlicensed use of her daughter's image, which appeared on T-shirts and other cheap products.

"We just don't want this to be a circus," said Debbie Almon, Baylee's grandmother.

windows during an explosion. The federal government made the decision that the new building would include no memorial to the Murrah victims.

"We really felt we needed to make a clear definition between the beginnings of the new building and the existing memorial," said project manager Tim Thury.

In 2001, Terry Nichols found out that law enforcement authorities planned the same fate for him that awaited McVeigh. Although he had been convicted of involuntary manslaughter and sentenced to life imprisonment by a federal judge, state prosecutors in Oklahoma said they planned to bring him to trial on 168 counts of murder. If convicted, Nichols could face the death penalty. Oklahoma City District Attorney Wes Lane said he was concerned that Nichols' federal conviction would be overturned on appeal, and that Nichols would go free.

"I simply don't know what might loom out there on the legal horizon which would place Terry Nichols' federal conviction in jeopardy," said Lane. "The interests

of the people of the state of Oklahoma cannot be vindi-cated by the blind reliance upon the federal government or Terry Lynn Nichols."

On July 13, 1999, as his appeals were running out, McVeigh was transported to the federal penitentiary in Terre Haute, Indiana, site of the federal government's execution chamber. On the grounds of the prison stood a small brick building, surrounded by chain-link fencing and razor wire. Inside the building was a raised, padded cot where the condemned man would be strapped to await lethal injection.

In late 2000, after the federal courts denied another round of McVeigh's appeals, he wrote Judge Matsch, informing him that he no longer planned to pursue appeals and that he was prepared to receive the sentence of the court. The federal Bureau of Prisons responded by scheduling McVeigh's execution for May 16, 2001.

As the day of the execution approached, there would

The federal government created a permanent memorial of the bombing with 168 bronze chairs, one for each victim. The government decided to erect a new building, but chose not to include a memorial because officials wanted to sym-bolize a new beginning.

be one final twist in the Oklahoma City bombing case. Just days before the execution, the F.B.I. revealed that it had found 3,135 documents generated by the investigation that had been withheld from McVeigh's lawyers. Under the rules of court, defense attorneys are entitled to see all evidence in the government's case against their clients. The process is known as "discovery."

Justice Department lawyers said there had been no plot to railroad McVeigh to the death chamber—that the documents had simply been misplaced, and they provided no evidence that would prove McVeigh's innocence. He had, after all, confessed many times to setting off the bomb. Still, U.S. Attorney General John Ashcroft decided to delay the execution to give McVeigh's lawyers as well as Judge Matsch a chance to review the documents.

"I believe the attorney general has a more important duty than the prosecution of any single case, as painful as that may be to our nation," said Ashcroft. "If any questions or doubts remain about this case, it would cast a permanent cloud over justice, diminishing its value and questioning its integrity."

After a month of poring over the documents, McVeigh's lawyers announced that the newly found records contained no evidence that would shed new light on the case. Most of the papers contained notes made by F.B.I. agents early in the investigation as they tracked down leads, most of which led nowhere.

McVeigh's execution was rescheduled for Monday, June 11, 2001.

At 4:10 A.M. on Sunday, June 10, McVeigh was taken from his cell at the Terre Haute jail and transferred to a 9-by-14-foot holding cell, just a short walk from the death chamber. That cell would be the place where McVeigh would spend his last full day on Earth. The cell has bare, tan walls; a narrow bed; a sink and toilet; a television; and a window that allows

guards in an adjacent room to watch the prisoner.

Rob Nigh, one of McVeigh's attorneys, walked with the condemned man as he was transferred across the prison yard to the brick building holding the cell and death chamber.

"He was able to look up in the sky and see the moon for the first time in a number of years," Nigh said.

At noon that day, McVeigh ate his last meal. He asked for two pints of mint chocolate chip ice cream.

Outside the prison, hundreds of people had arrived. Many of them were morally opposed to the death penalty and had come to Terre Haute to protest against the execution.

The antideath penalty advocates staged a three-mile march from a Terre Haute church to the prison. They carried signs that said "Don't Kill for Me" and "Thou Shalt Not Kill." Some protesters carried huge papier-mâché sculptures of Uncle Sam and Jesus Christ inscribed with antideath penalty messages.

Antideath penalty protestors congregate outside the United States Penitentiary in Terre Haute, Indiana, the day before Timothy McVeigh's execution. Protestors staged a three-mile march against the death penalty.

One of the protesters was Suzanne Carter, president of an antideath penalty group known as the Terre Haute Abolition Network. She told a reporter: "I wish we weren't doing this. I wish this wasn't happening. I wish we were getting together to celebrate abolition" of the death penalty.

Another protester was Carolyn Gray, who drove up to Terre Haute from Jupiter, Florida, to be part of the anti-death penalty march.

"When the government sets an example by killing its own citizens, it sends out a message that it's okay to kill," said Gray. "It shows a lack of respect for life and it copies the act of the killer."

A much smaller group gathered nearby to support the execution. Two of the prodeath penalty activists were Martha and Thad Brown, who arrived at a rally in Terre Haute's Vorhees Park to find a group of just 10 people supporting the execution.

"My husband and I decided we had to join them and add to their support," Martha Brown said. "I felt I needed to do this. I had to do this for the 168 people who died in Oklahoma."

Back in Oklahoma City, the Justice Department made arrangements so the survivors and family members of the victims could watch the execution on a closed-circuit telecast. Monitors were set up in a conference room of a federal detention center, where 232 survivors and family members gathered to watch the execution.

Just before 7 A.M. on June 11, McVeigh was led from the detention cell to the death chamber. He was dressed in a white T-shirt, khaki prison-issue pants and slip-on sneakers. His hair was shaved to a bristle.

Prison officials told McVeigh, a Catholic, that a minister was available to administer Last Rites.

"Sure, send him in," McVeigh said.

Bill McVeigh, Timothy's father, removes the flag from his lawn days before his son's execution. McVeigh had flown the flag in support of his country, but said "I ain't gonna have it up when Tim loses his life."

The Reverend Frank Roof, the prison chaplain, entered the death chamber and performed the short religious ritual for the condemned man.

Next, McVeigh lay down on the gurney. His arms were fastened by Velcro straps. A white sheet was pulled up to his chin. Finally, a technician pierced a vein in his leg with a surgical needle, fastening it to an intravenous tube. Above the gurney, trained on McVeigh's face, was a T.V. camera sending the image to the audience in Oklahoma City.

Harley Lapin, warden of the Terre Haute penitentiary stepped forward. He said, "Inmate McVeigh, you may make your final statement."

McVeigh chose to remain silent.

"It was the quietest moment through the whole process," said Crocker Stephenson, a newspaper reporter selected to witness the execution.

Next, U.S. Marshal Frank Anderson reached for the receiver of a red telephone sitting on a steel table in the death chamber. It was Anderson's job to check whether a last-minute stay of execution had been granted by President Bush or a Supreme Court justice. There would be no stay issued in this case. After the short call, Anderson hung up the receiver and said, "We may proceed."

At 7:08 A.M., the flow of chemicals into McVeigh's bloodstream commenced. The first solution to enter his body was sodium pentothal, a drug that would sedate McVeigh.

After two minutes, pancuronium bromide was released. It is a muscle relaxant, intended to collapse the diaphragm and lungs. Witnesses reported that McVeigh's breathing grew labored, his lips fluttered and turned blue, and his eyes appeared to roll back in his head.

Finally, at 7:13 A.M., potassium chloride entered McVeigh's blood. The drug stopped McVeigh's heart. McVeigh's lips parted, and it appeared to witnesses that his skin took on a yellowish tone.

At 7:14 A.M. on June 11, 2001—some six years after a bomb destroyed the Murrah federal building in Oklahoma City—Timothy McVeigh was declared dead.

Ten survivors and family members from Oklahoma City had traveled to Terre Haute, and were given permission to witness the execution.

"All 168 victims were there with us in that room," said Kay Fulton, whose brother died in the blast.

Shortly before he was led into the death chamber,

McVeigh sat down and wrote out the words of the William Ernest Henley poem "Invictus." Henley had overcome a lot in his life—the loss of his right leg, poverty, the early death of his father—to achieve success as a journalist and writer in Victorian England. The poem, which Henley wrote in 1875, is an ode to the strength of spirit.

McVeigh asked that reporters be given a copy of the words following his death, and prison officials obliged.

By choosing Henley's words, McVeigh make it clear that he believed in his twisted, violent cause to the end.

The poem concludes:

It matters not how strait the gate,
How charged with punishments the scroll,
I am the master of my fate:
I am the captain of my soul.

Family members of Dolores Stratton, a victim of the 1995 bombing, wipe away tears as they watch Timothy McVeigh's execution on closed-circuit television. Nearly 300 people turned out for the private viewing.

Chronology

1968   Timothy McVeigh born near Buffalo, New York.

1972   U.S. Supreme Court rules the death penalty unconstitutional; states rewrite their capital punishment laws to conform with the court's order.

1977   Convicted killer Gary Gilmore executed in Utah, ending a 10-year moratorium on capital punishment in the United States.

1988   McVeigh and Terry Nichols enlist in the U.S. Army.

1989   Nichols leaves the Army.

1991   McVeigh serves in the Persian Gulf War, then leaves the Army.

1992   Federal agents kill wife and son of white separatist Randy Weaver in a shoot-out in Ruby Ridge, Idaho.

1993   Federal agents storm the compound of the Branch Davidian religious cult near Waco, Texas. During the siege, a fire erupts in the compound, taking the lives of 86 Branch Davidians, including 17 children.

1994   To raise money for the bombing of the Murrah building, McVeigh, Nichols, and Michael Fortier steal $60,000 from a gun dealer in Arkansas.

1995   On April 19, a bomb explodes outside the Alfred P. Murrah Federal Building in Oklahoma City, Oklahoma; 168 people, including 19 children, are killed when the front half of the building collapses. In August, McVeigh and Nichols are indicted for constructing a weapon of mass destruction.

1997   McVeigh is convicted in June of igniting the bomb at the Murrah building and sentenced to death; Nichols is convicted in December of involuntary manslaughter and sentenced to life imprisonment.

1999   Students Dylan Klebold and Eric Harris murder 13 people at Columbine High School in Colorado with weapons obtained at a gun show.

2000   McVeigh gives up his appeals.

2001   McVeigh is executed by lethal injection in June. In September, more than 3,000 people are killed when terrorists use hijacked jet planes to crash into the World Trade Center in New York City and the Pentagon in Washington D.C.

Bibliography

Bacharach, Phil. "The Prison Letters of Timothy McVeigh." *Esquire*, May 2001.

Bohrer, David. *America's Special Forces*. Osceola, Wisconsin: MBI Publishing Co., 1998.

Bush, George W. "Remarks on the Execution of Timothy McVeigh." Superintendent of Documents, U.S. Government Printing Office, June 11, 2001.

Cohen, Sharon. "Counting Down the Final Hours." Associated Press, June 11, 2001.

Cole, Michael D. *The Siege at Waco: Deadly Inferno*. Springfield, N.J.: Enslow Publishing, 1999.

Cole, Patrick E. "I'm Just Like Anyone Else." *Time,* April 15, 1996.

Daley, Bill. "Oklahoma Survivor Ready to Move On." *The Hartford Courant,* June 14, 2001.

Dempsey, Jim. "'Invictus' has the Power that Lasts, Poet's Reply to Sorrow Illustrates True Strength." Worcester, Mass., *Telegram and Gazette,* June 15, 2001.

Douglas, John, and Olshaker, Mark. *The Anatomy of Motive*. New York: Lisa Drew-Scribner, 1999.

Espo, David. "Bush Vows Justice." Associated Press, Sept. 21, 2001.

Farley, Christopher John. "America's Bomb Culture." *Time,* May 8, 1995.

Gibbs, Nancy. "Botching the Big Case." *Time,* May 21, 2001.

Gleick, Elizabeth. "Something Big is Going to Happen." *Time,* May 8, 1995.

Gleick, Elizabeth. "Living with the Nightmares." *Time,* April 15, 1996.

Hathaway, Jason. "Don't Kill for Me." *Terre Haute Tribune Star,* June 11, 2001.

Jones, Stephen, and Israel, Peter. *Others Unknown: The Oklahoma City Bombing Case and Conspiracy*. New York: Perseus Books Group, 1998.

Kennedy, Helen; Ingrassia, Robert; and Siemaszko, Corky. "Bomber Remains Silent, Unrepentant to the Very End." *New York Daily News,* June 12, 2001.

Bibliography

Kennedy, Helen. "They Watched as He Took His Last Breath." *New York Daily News,* June 12, 2001.

Lacayo, Richard. "A Moment of Silence." *Time,* May 8, 1995.

Lacayo, Richard. "The State Versus McVeigh." *Time,* April 15, 1996.

Long, Robert Emmet. *Religious Cults in America.* New York: H.W. Wilson Company, 1994.

Marcovitz, Hal. *Terrorism.* Philadelphia: Chelsea House Publishers, 2001.

McRoberts, Flynn, and Murr, Andrew. "I Thought I Was Going to Die." *Newsweek,* June 18, 2001.

Michel, Lou, and Herbeck, Dan. *American Terrorist: Timothy McVeigh and the Oklahoma City Bombing.* New York: HarperCollins Publishers, 2001.

Moore, Robin. *The Green Berets.* New York: Crown Publishers Inc., 1965.

Nash, Jay Robert. *Terrorism in the 20th Century.* New York: M. Evans and Co. Inc., 1998.

Pastore, Patricia L. "Demonstrators Pray for McVeigh, Victims' Families." *Terre Haute Tribune Star,* June 11, 2001.

Prodis, Julia. "Four Lives." Associated Press, April 17, 1996.

Serrano, Richard A. *One of Ours: Timothy McVeigh and the Oklahoma City Bombing.* New York: W.W. Norton and Co., 1998.

Smolowe, Jill. "Enemies of the State." *Time,* May 8, 1995.

Stickney, Brandon M. *All-American Monster: The Unauthorized Biography of Timothy McVeigh.* New York: Prometheus Books, 1996.

Tally, Tim. "Bomb Conspirator Could Face Death." Associated Press, Sept, 6, 2001.

Tomaso, Bruce. "Drama Takes Unusual Twists: Sect's Ex-Leader Denounces Koresh." *The Dallas Morning News,* March 3, 1993.

Wagner, Dennis. "Legislation Considered for Gun Shows." *The Arizona Republic,* Feb. 11, 2000.

Wecht, Cyril. *Grave Secrets.* New York: Dutton, 1996.

Wilson-Smith, Anthony. "No Safe Place." *McLean's,* May 1, 1995.

"A Bittersweet Win for Photographer." Associated Press, April 10, 1996.

"A Covenant With Death - Timothy McVeigh's Execution." *The Economist,* May 12, 2001.

"Work Starts on New Oklahoma City Federal Building." Associated Press, June 15, 2001.

World Wide Web

Gary Gilmore
http://www.quoteland.com

History of the Death Penalty
http://www.uaa.alaska.edu/just/death/history.html
http://www.deathpenaltyinfor.org/history2.html
#TheDeathPenaltyinAmerica

History of the Second Amendment. David E. Vandercoy. Valparaiso University Law Review
http://www.2ndlawlib.org/journals/vandhist.html

History of the Second Amendment. Carl T. Bogus. Roger Williams University School of Law
http://www.vpc.org/fact_sht/hidhist.htm

The Bradley Fighting Vehicle
http://www.fas.org/man/dod-101/sys/land/m2.htm

Michelle Rauch's Testimony in Oklahoma Bombing Trial
http://www.okcitytrial.com/content/dailytx/061097p/
MichelleRauchDirectExamina.html

Tragedy at Columbine High School. Boulder Daily Camera
http://www.thedailycamera.com

Further Reading

Bohrer, David. *America's Special Forces.* Osceola, Wisconsin: MBI Publishing Co., 1998.

Cole, Michael D. *The Siege at Waco: Deadly Inferno.* Springfield, N.J.: Enslow Publishing, 1999.

Douglas, John, and Olshaker, Mark. *The Anatomy of Motive.* New York: Lisa Drew-Scribner, 1999.

Jones, Stephen, and Israel, Peter. *Others Unknown: The Oklahoma City Bombing Case and Conspiracy.* New York: Perseus Books Group, 1998.

Long, Robert Emmet. *Religious Cults in America.* New York: H.W. Wilson Company, 1994.

Marcovitz, Hal. *Terrorism.* Philadelphia: Chelsea House Publishers, 2001.

Michel, Lou, and Herbeck, Dan. *American Terrorist: Timothy McVeigh and the Oklahoma City Bombing.* New York: HarperCollins Publishers, 2001.

Moore, Robin. *The Green Berets.* New York: Crown Publishers Inc., 1965.

Nash, Jay Robert. *Terrorism in the 20th Century.* New York: M. Evans and Co. Inc., 1998.

Serrano, Richard A. *One of Ours: Timothy McVeigh and the Oklahoma City Bombing.* New York: W.W. Norton and Co., 1998.

Stickney, Brandon M. *All-American Monster: The Unauthorized Biography of Timothy McVeigh.* New York: Prometheus Books, 1996.

Wecht, Cyril. *Grave Secrets.* New York: Dutton, 1996.

Index

Index

Index

HAL MARCOVITZ is a journalist for *The Morning Call*, a newspaper based in Allentown, Pennsylvania. He has written more than 30 books for young readers. His other titles for the Great Disasters series include *Terrorism* and *The Munich Olympics*. He lives in Chalfont, Pennsylvania, with his wife Gail and daughters Ashley and Michelle.

JILL McCAFFREY has served for four years as national chairman of the Armed Forces Emergency Services of the American Red Cross. Ms. McCaffrey also serves on the board of directors for Knollwood—the Army Distaff Hall. The former Jill Ann Faulkner, a Massachusetts native, is the wife of Barry R. McCaffrey, who served in President Bill Clinton's cabinet as director of the White House Office of National Drug Control Policy. The McCaffreys are the parents of three grown children: Sean, a major in the U.S. Army; Tara, an intensive care nurse and captain in the National Guard; and Amy, a seventh grade teacher. The McCaffreys also have two grandchildren, Michael and Jack.

Picture Credits